everyday
italian

Bath · New York · Cologne · Melbourne · Delhi
Hong Kong · Shenzhen · Singapore

This edition published by Parragon in 2016

Parragon
Chartist House
15-17 Trim Street
Bath BA1 1HA, UK
www.parragon.com

ISBN 978-1-4075-2800-7

Printed in China

Created and produced by Terry Jeavons & Company

This book uses both metric and imperial measurements. Follow the same units of measurement throughout; do not mix metric and imperial. All spoon measurements are level: teaspoons are assumed to be 5ml, and tablespoons are assumed to be 15ml. Unless otherwise stated, milk is assumed to be full fat, eggs and individual vegetables are medium, and pepper is freshly ground black pepper.

Recipes using raw or very lightly cooked eggs should be avoided by infants, the elderly, pregnant women, convalescents and anyone suffering from an illness. Pregnant and breastfeeding women are advised to avoid eating peanuts and peanut products. Sufferers from nut allergies should be aware that some of the ready-made ingredients used in the recipes in this book may contain nuts. Always check the packaging before use.

Vegetarians should be aware that some of the ready-made ingredients used in the recipes in this book may contain animal products. Always check the packaging before use.

everyday
italian

introduction

At the heart of Italian cuisine lies a very special ingredient – the legendary Italian love of good things, including good food. Learning the skills of cooking begins at an early age, as recipes and techniques are handed down the generations, and so too does an appreciation of well-prepared meals, whether a plate of *al dente* pasta topped with a simple sauce of freshly picked tomatoes, an aromatic beef stew or a perfect seafood risotto.

It is often said that the essence of Italian cooking can be summed up in two words – seasonal and regional. Italians respect their ingredients and insist on the best quality, so they prefer to use

seasonal produce that, if possible, is locally grown. In provincial towns and villages, people shop daily for fresh produce in the markets and plan the menu for that day around whichever ingredients feel, smell and look to be in peak condition.

This emphasis has had a lasting effect on the style of Italian cuisine, and simplicity is the key word. But simplicity means something different in each region of Italy. The reason for this is a mix of geographical and cultural diversity. The north of the country is cooler and wetter, while the south is hotter and drier, and the crops reflect this. In the north, dairy farming produces butter, cream and cheese, which feature widely in the region's traditonal cooking, and both rice and maize are cultivated here, so risotto and polenta are staples. The south, on the other hand, is the home of pasta, olives and olive oil, tomatoes, aubergines and citrus fruits.

The cultural differences arise from the fact that Italy has only

relatively recently become a unified country, created from a number of independent states each with their own traditions, to which they adhere fiercely. This is perhaps part of the irresistible appeal of Italian cuisine – but whatever the reason, embrace it and enjoy it!

starters,
soups & salads

Soups are usually served as the first course of an Italian dinner, and they are so hearty and delicious that they also make excellent light lunch or supper dishes. Vegetables are the main ingredients of a good Italian soup, which sometimes has tiny soup pasta or rice added, occasionally a little meat, and frequently a selection of fish and seafood. The Italians are creative when it comes to adapting their soup recipes to include whatever vegetables are in season, and you can be, too.

If the soups are a visual feast, so too are the antipasti. They are a tasty, light, appetizing way to start a meal, consisting mainly of cured meats, vegetables, seafood, cheese and salads. The ingredients are simple but the combinations effective – the Three-colour Salad of fresh sliced tomatoes, buffalo mozzarella and fragrant basil leaves is made in moments, and the superb Italian cured ham, prosciutto, is wonderful served with fresh fruit, such as melon or figs, or salad leaves such as rocket.

Olive oil makes a frequent appearance in the ingredients list for antipasti – save your best bottle of extra virgin olive oil for dressing salads or 'drizzling' on hot dishes, as the excellent flavour will really enhance an authentic Italian dish. The slightly more acidic virgin olive oil can be used for cooking.

fresh tomato soup

ingredients

SERVES 4

1 tbsp olive oil

650 g/1 lb 7 oz plum
tomatoes

1 onion, cut into quarters

1 garlic clove, thinly sliced

1 celery stick, roughly
chopped

500 ml/18 fl oz chicken stock

55 g/2 oz dried anellini or
other soup pasta

salt and pepper

fresh flat-leaf parsley,
chopped, to garnish

method

1 Pour the olive oil into a large heavy-based
saucepan and add the tomatoes, onion, garlic
and celery. Cover and cook over a low heat for
45 minutes, occasionally shaking the pan
gently, until the mixture is pulpy.

2 Transfer the mixture to a food processor or
blender and process to a smooth purée. Push
the purée through a sieve into a clean pan.

3 Add the stock and bring to the boil. Add
the pasta, bring back to the boil and cook for
8–10 minutes, until the pasta is tender but still
firm to the bite. Season to taste with salt and
pepper. Ladle into warmed bowls, sprinkle
with the parsley and serve immediately.

minestrone

ingredients

SERVES 4

3 tbsp olive oil

2 onions, chopped

1/2 small green or Savoy
cabbage, thick stems
removed and leaves
shredded

2 courgettes, chopped

2 celery sticks, chopped

2 carrots, chopped

2 potatoes, chopped

4 large tomatoes, peeled
and chopped

115 g/4 oz dried cannellini
beans, soaked overnight
in enough cold water to
cover

1.2 litres/2 pints chicken or
vegetable stock

115 g/4 oz dried soup pasta

salt and pepper

freshly shaved Parmesan
cheese, to garnish

4 tbsp freshly grated
Parmesan cheese,
to serve

method

1 Heat the oil in a large heavy-based saucepan.
Add the onions and cook over a low heat,
stirring occasionally, for 5 minutes, or until
softened.

2 Add the cabbage, courgettes, celery, carrots,
potatoes and tomatoes to the pan, cover and
cook, stirring occasionally, for 10 minutes.

3 Drain and rinse the beans, then add to the
pan. Pour in the stock, bring to the boil, cover
and simmer for 1–1 1/2 hours, or until the
beans are tender.

4 Add the soup pasta to the pan and cook,
uncovered, for 8–10 minutes, or until tender
but still firm to the bite. Season to taste with
salt and pepper and ladle into warmed bowls.
Garnish with fresh Parmesan cheese shavings
and an extra sprinkling of pepper. Serve
immediately, handing around the grated
Parmesan cheese separately.

beef soup with eggs

ingredients

SERVES 4

consommé

500 g/1 lb 2 oz beef marrow
    bones, sawn into 7.5-cm/
    3-inch pieces
350 g/12 oz stewing beef, in
    one piece
1.4 litres /2½ pints water
4 cloves
2 onions, halved
2 celery sticks, roughly
    chopped
8 peppercorns
1 bouquet garni

topping

55 g/2 oz unsalted butter
4 slices fresh white bread
115 g/4 oz freshly grated
    Parmesan cheese
4 eggs
salt and pepper

method

1 First, make the consommé. Place the bones
in a large heavy-based saucepan with the
stewing beef on top. Add the water and bring
to the boil over a low heat, skimming off all
the scum that rises to the surface. Pierce
each onion half with a clove and add to the
pan with the celery, peppercorns and bouquet
garni. Partially cover and simmer very gently
for 3 hours. Remove the meat and simmer
for a further hour.

2 Strain the consommé into a bowl and set
aside to cool. When completely cool, chill in
the refrigerator for at least 6 hours, preferably
overnight. Carefully remove and discard the
layer of fat that has formed on the surface.
Return the consommé to a clean pan and
heat until almost boiling.

3 When you are ready to serve, melt the butter
in a heavy-based frying pan. Add the bread,
1 slice at a time if necessary, and cook over a
medium heat until crisp and golden on both
sides. Remove from the pan and place one slice
in the base of each of 4 warmed soup bowls.

4 Sprinkle half the Parmesan over the fried
bread. Carefully break an egg over each slice
of fried bread, keeping the yolks whole. Season
to taste with salt and pepper and sprinkle with
the remaining Parmesan. Carefully ladle the
hot consommé into the soup bowls and
serve immediately.

white bean soup

ingredients

SERVES 4

175 g/6 oz dried cannellini
    beans, covered and
    soaked overnight in cold
    water
1.7 litres/3 pints chicken or
    vegetable stock
115 g/4 oz dried corallini,
    conchigliette piccole
    or other soup pasta
6 tbsp olive oil
2 garlic cloves, finely
    chopped
4 tbsp chopped fresh flat-leaf
    parsley
salt and pepper

method

1 Drain the soaked beans and place them in a large heavy-based saucepan. Add the stock and bring to the boil. Partially cover the pan, reduce the heat and simmer for 2 hours, until tender.

2 Transfer about half the beans and a little of the stock to a food processor or blender and process to a smooth purée. Return the purée to the pan and stir well to mix. Bring the soup back to the boil.

3 Add the pasta to the soup, bring back to the boil and cook for 10 minutes, until tender.

4 Meanwhile, heat 4 tablespoons of the olive oil in a small saucepan. Add the garlic and cook over a low heat, stirring frequently, for 4–5 minutes, until golden. Stir the garlic into the soup and add the parsley. Season to taste with salt and pepper and ladle into warmed soup bowls. Drizzle with the remaining olive oil and serve immediately.

genoese vegetable soup

ingredients

SERVES 8

2 onions, sliced

2 carrots, diced

2 celery sticks, sliced

2 potatoes, diced

115 g/4 oz French beans, cut
into 2.5-cm/1-inch lengths

115 g/4 oz peas

200 g/7 oz fresh young
spinach leaves, shredded

2 courgettes, diced

225 g/8 oz plum tomatoes,
peeled, deseeded
and diced

3 garlic cloves, thinly sliced

4 tbsp extra virgin olive oil

2 litres/3^1/$_2$ pints
vegetable stock

salt and pepper

140 g/5 oz dried soup pasta

freshly grated Parmesan
cheese, to serve

pesto

4 tbsp fresh basil leaves

1 tbsp pine kernels

1 garlic clove

25 g/1 oz freshly grated
Parmesan cheese

3 tbsp extra virgin olive oil

method

1 Put the onions, carrots, celery, potatoes, beans, peas, spinach, courgettes, tomatoes and garlic in a large heavy-based saucepan, pour in the olive oil and stock and bring to the boil over a medium–low heat. Reduce the heat and simmer gently for about 1^1/$_2$ hours.

2 Meanwhile, make the pesto. Put the basil, pine kernels and garlic into a mortar and pound to a paste with a pestle. Transfer to a bowl and gradually work in the Parmesan with a wooden spoon, followed by the olive oil to make a thick, creamy sauce. Cover with clingfilm and set aside in the refrigerator until required.

3 Season the soup to taste with salt and pepper and add the pasta. Cook for a further 8–10 minutes, until the pasta is tender but still firm to the bite. The soup should be very thick.

4 Stir in half the pesto, remove the pan from the heat and set aside to rest for 4 minutes. Taste and adjust the seasoning, adding more salt, pepper and pesto if necessary. (Any leftover pesto may be stored in a screw-top jar in the refrigerator for up to 2 weeks.) Ladle into warmed bowls and serve immediately. Pass round the freshly grated Parmesan cheese separately.

mixed antipasto meat platter

ingredients

SERVES 4

1 cantaloupe melon

55 g/2 oz Italian salami, thinly sliced

8 slices prosciutto

8 slices bresaola

8 slices mortadella

4 plum tomatoes, thinly sliced

4 fresh figs, quartered

115 g/4 oz black olives, stoned and sliced

2 tbsp shredded fresh basil leaves

4 tbsp extra virgin olive oil, plus extra for serving

pepper

method

1 Cut the melon in half, scoop out and discard the seeds, then cut the flesh into 8 wedges. Arrange the wedges on one half of a large serving platter.

2 Arrange the salami, prosciutto, bresaola and mortadella in loose folds on the other half of the platter. Arrange the tomato slices and fig quarters along the centre of the platter.

3 Sprinkle the olives over the meat. Sprinkle the basil over the tomatoes and drizzle with olive oil. Season to taste with pepper, then serve with extra olive oil.

marinated raw beef

ingredients

SERVES 4

200 g/7 oz fillet steak, in one
    piece
2 tbsp lemon juice
salt and pepper
4 tbsp extra virgin olive oil
55 g/2 oz Parmesan cheese,
    thinly shaved
4 tbsp chopped fresh flat-leaf
    parsley
lemon slices, to garnish
ciabatta or focaccia, to serve

method

1 Using a very sharp knife, cut the fillet steak into wafer-thin slices and arrange on 4 individual serving plates.

2 Pour the lemon juice into a small bowl and season to taste with salt and pepper. Whisk in the olive oil, then pour the dressing over the meat. Cover the plates with clingfilm and set aside for 10–15 minutes to marinate.

3 Remove and discard the clingfilm. Arrange the Parmesan shavings in the centre of each serving and sprinkle with parsley. Garnish with lemon slices and serve with fresh bread.

parma ham & figs

ingredients

SERVES 4

175 g/6 oz prosciutto,
    thinly sliced

pepper

4 fresh figs

1 lime

2 fresh basil sprigs

method

1 Using a sharp knife, trim the visible fat from the slices of prosciutto and discard. Arrange the prosciutto on 4 large serving plates, loosely folding it so that it falls into decorative shapes. Season to taste with pepper.

2 Using a sharp knife, cut each fig lengthways into four wedges. Arrange a fig on each serving plate. Cut the lime into 6 wedges, place a wedge on each plate and reserve the others. Remove the leaves from the basil sprigs and divide between the plates. Cover with clingfilm and chill in the refrigerator until ready to serve.

3 Just before serving, remove the plates from the refrigerator and squeeze the juice from the remaining lime wedges over the ham.

prosciutto with rocket

ingredients

SERVES 4

115 g/4 oz rocket
1 tbsp lemon juice
salt and pepper
3 tbsp extra virgin olive oil
225 g/8 oz prosciutto, thinly
    sliced

method

1 Separate the rocket leaves, wash in cold water and pat dry on kitchen paper. Place the leaves in a bowl.

2 Pour the lemon juice into a small bowl and season to taste with salt and pepper. Whisk in the olive oil, then pour the dressing over the rocket leaves and toss lightly so they are evenly coated.

3 Carefully drape the prosciutto in folds on individual serving plates, then add the rocket. Serve at room temperature.

chicken crostini

ingredients

SERVES 4

12 slices French bread
   or rustic bread
4 tbsp olive oil
2 garlic cloves, chopped
2 tbsp finely chopped fresh
   oregano
salt and pepper
100 g/3½ oz cold roast
   chicken, cut into small,
   thin slices
4 tomatoes, sliced
12 thin slices of goat's cheese
12 black olives, stoned and
   chopped
fresh red and green lettuce
   leaves, to serve

method

1 Preheat the grill to medium. Put the bread under the grill and lightly toast on both sides. Meanwhile, pour the olive oil into a bowl and add the garlic and oregano. Season with salt and pepper and mix well. Remove the toasted bread slices from the grill and brush them on one side only with the oil mixture.

2 Place the bread slices, oiled sides up, on a baking sheet. Put some sliced chicken on top of each one, followed by a slice of tomato. Divide the slices of goat's cheese between them, then top with the chopped olives.

3 Drizzle over the remaining oil mixture and transfer to a preheated oven, 180°C/350°F/ Gas Mark 4. Bake for about 5 minutes, or until the cheese is golden and starting to melt. Remove from the oven and serve on a bed of fresh red and green lettuce leaves.

warm vegetable medley

ingredients

SERVES 4

4 tbsp olive oil

2 celery sticks, sliced

2 red onions, sliced

450 g/1 lb aubergine, diced

1 garlic clove, finely chopped

5 plum tomatoes, chopped

3 tbsp red wine vinegar

1 tbsp sugar

3 tbsp green olives, stoned

2 tbsp capers

salt and pepper

4 tbsp chopped fresh flat-leaf
    parsley

ciabatta or panini, to serve

method

1 Heat half the olive oil in a large heavy-based saucepan. Add the celery and onions and cook over a low heat, stirring occasionally, for 5 minutes, until softened but not coloured. Add the remaining oil and the aubergine. Cook, stirring frequently, for about 5 minutes, until the aubergine starts to colour.

2 Add the garlic, tomatoes, vinegar and sugar, and mix well. Cover the mixture with a circle of waxed paper and simmer gently for about 10 minutes.

3 Remove the waxed paper, stir in the olives and capers and season to taste with salt and pepper. Pour the vegetables into a serving dish and set aside to cool to room temperature. Sprinkle the parsley over the vegetables and serve with fresh bread or rolls.

sicilian stuffed tomatoes

ingredients

SERVES 4

8 large, ripe tomatoes

7 tbsp extra virgin olive oil

2 onions, finely chopped

2 garlic cloves, crushed

115 g/4 oz fresh
    breadcrumbs

8 anchovy fillets in oil,
    drained and chopped

3 tbsp black olives, stoned
    and chopped

2 tbsp chopped fresh flat-leaf
    parsley

1 tbsp chopped fresh oregano

4 tbsp freshly grated
    Parmesan cheese

method

1 Cut a thin slice off the tops of the tomatoes and discard. Scoop out the seeds with a teaspoon and discard, taking care not to pierce the shells. Turn the tomato shells upside down on kitchen paper to drain.

2 Heat 6 tablespoons of the olive oil in a frying pan, add the onions and garlic and cook over a low heat, stirring occasionally, for 5 minutes, until softened. Remove the pan from the heat and stir in the breadcrumbs, anchovies, olives and herbs.

3 Using a teaspoon, fill the tomato shells with the breadcrumb mixture, then place in an ovenproof dish large enough to hold them in a single layer. Sprinkle the tops with grated Parmesan and drizzle with the remaining oil.

4 Bake in a preheated oven, 180°C/350°F/Gas Mark 4, for 20–25 minutes, until the tomatoes are tender and the topping is golden brown.

5 Remove the dish from the oven and serve immediately, if serving hot, or allow to cool to room temperature.

roman artichokes

ingredients

SERVES 4

5 tbsp lemon juice

4 globe artichokes

2 garlic cloves, 1 whole and 1
    finely chopped

4 sprigs fresh flat-leaf parsley

2 sprigs fresh mint

1 lemon, quartered

4 tbsp olive oil

salt and pepper

2 tbsp dry, uncoloured
    breadcrumbs

2 tbsp fresh flat-leaf parsley,
    roughly chopped

2 tbsp fresh mint,
    roughly chopped

1 tbsp unsalted butter, diced

method

1 Fill a large bowl with cold water and
4 tablespoons of the lemon juice. Snap the stem
off one artichoke, then peel away the tough
outer leaves. Snip off the tough tops of the
remaining leaves. Cut off the top 2 cm/3/4 inch
of the central cone with a sharp knife. Drop the
artichoke into the bowl and prepare the others.

2 Wedge the artichokes firmly upright in a
single layer in a heavy-based saucepan. Add
the whole garlic clove, parsley and mint sprigs,
lemon, oil and seasoning. Add water to come
two thirds of the way up the sides. Bring to
the boil over a low heat, cover and simmer
for 15 minutes, until nearly tender.

3 Combine the breadcrumbs with the chopped
garlic, parsley and mint in a bowl, and season.

4 Remove the artichokes from the pan. When
cool, gently separate the leaves, then remove
the central cones with a teaspoon and discard.
Season the artichokes to taste and return to the
pan. Spoon the breadcrumb mixture into the
centres, cover tightly and cook over a low heat
for 20–30 minutes, until tender. Remove with
a slotted spoon and place on 4 individual plates.

5 Strain the cooking liquid into a clean saucepan
and bring to the boil. Cook until the liquid is
concentrated, then reduce the heat and stir in
the remaining lemon juice. Swirl in the butter,
a piece at a time. Do not let the sauce boil.
Serve the artichokes warm with the sauce.

pasta salad with chargrilled peppers

ingredients

SERVES 4

1 red pepper

1 orange pepper

280 g/10 oz dried conchiglie

5 tbsp extra virgin olive oil

2 tbsp lemon juice

2 tbsp pesto (see page 16)

1 garlic clove

3 tbsp shredded fresh basil
  leaves

salt and pepper

method

1 Put the whole peppers on a baking sheet and place under a preheated grill, turning frequently, for 15 minutes, until charred all over. Remove with tongs and place in a bowl. Cover with crumpled kitchen paper and set aside.

2 Meanwhile, bring a large saucepan of lightly salted water to the boil. Add the pasta, bring back to the boil and cook for 8–10 minutes, until tender but still firm to the bite.

3 Combine the olive oil, lemon juice, pesto and garlic in a bowl, whisking well to mix. Drain the pasta, add it to the pesto mixture while still hot and toss well. Set aside.

4 When the peppers are cool enough to handle, peel off the skins, then cut open and remove the seeds. Roughly chop the flesh and add it to the pasta with the basil. Season to taste with salt and pepper and toss well. Serve at room temperature.

warm pasta salad

ingredients

SERVES 4

225 g/8 oz dried farfalle or
other pasta shapes
6 pieces of sun-dried tomato
in oil, drained and
chopped
4 spring onions, chopped
55 g/2 oz rocket, shredded
1/2 cucumber, deseeded and
diced
salt and pepper
2 tbsp freshly grated
Parmesan cheese

dressing

4 tbsp olive oil
1/2 tsp caster sugar
1 tbsp white wine vinegar
1 tsp Dijon mustard
salt and pepper
4 fresh basil leaves,
finely shredded

method

1 To make the dressing, whisk the olive oil, sugar, vinegar and mustard together in a bowl. Season to taste with salt and pepper. Stir in the basil.

2 Bring a large heavy-based saucepan of lightly salted water to the boil. Add the pasta, return to the boil and cook for 8–10 minutes, or until tender but still firm to the bite. Drain and transfer to a salad bowl. Add the dressing and toss well.

3 Add the sun-dried tomatoes, spring onions, rocket and cucumber, season to taste with salt and pepper, and toss. Sprinkle with the Parmesan cheese and serve warm.

layered tomato salad

ingredients

SERVES 4

1 red onion, thinly sliced
into rings

4 slices day-old bread

450 g/1 lb tomatoes, thinly
sliced

115 g/4 oz buffalo mozzarella,
thinly sliced

1 tbsp shredded fresh basil

salt and pepper

125 ml/4 fl oz extra virgin
olive oil

3 tbsp balsamic vinegar

4 tbsp lemon juice

115 g/4 oz black olives,
stoned and thinly sliced

method

1 Place the onion slices in a bowl and add cold water to cover. Set aside to soak for 10 minutes. Meanwhile, dip the slices of bread in a shallow dish of cold water, then squeeze out the excess. Place the bread in a serving dish.

2 Drain the onion slices and layer them on the bread with the tomatoes and mozzarella, sprinkling each layer with the basil and salt and pepper.

3 Pour over the olive oil, vinegar and lemon juice and sprinkle with the sliced olives. Cover with clingfilm and chill for up to 8 hours before serving.

three-colour salad

ingredients

SERVES 4

280 g/10 oz buffalo
   mozzarella, drained and
   thinly sliced

8 plum tomatoes, sliced

salt and pepper

20 fresh basil leaves

125 ml/4 fl oz extra virgin
   olive oil

method

1 Arrange the cheese and tomato slices on 4 individual serving plates and season to taste with salt. Set aside in a cool place for 30 minutes.

2 Sprinkle the basil leaves over the salad and drizzle with the olive oil. Season with pepper and serve immediately.

mozzarella salad
with sun-dried tomatoes

ingredients

SERVES 4

140 g/5 oz sun-dried
   tomatoes in olive oil
   (drained weight), reserving
   the oil from the bottle
1 tbsp fresh basil, roughly
   shredded
1 tbsp fresh flat-leaf parsley,
   roughly chopped
1 tbsp capers, rinsed
1 tbsp balsamic vinegar
1 garlic clove, roughly
   chopped
extra olive oil, if necessary
pepper
100 g/3½ oz mixed salad
   leaves, such as oak leaf
   lettuce, baby spinach
   and rocket
500 g/1 lb 2 oz smoked
   mozzarella, sliced

method

1 Put the sun-dried tomatoes, basil, parsley,
capers, vinegar and garlic in a food processor
or blender. Measure the oil from the sun-dried
tomatoes jar and add in enough olive oil to
make 150 ml/5 fl oz. Add it to the food processor
or blender and process until smooth. Season to
taste with pepper.

2 Divide the salad leaves between 4 individual
serving plates. Top with the slices of mozzarella
and spoon the dressing over them. Serve
immediately.

artichoke & rocket salad

ingredients

SERVES 4

8 baby globe artichokes

juice of 2 lemons

bunch of rocket

125 ml/4 fl oz extra virgin
    olive oil

salt and pepper

115 g/4 oz pecorino cheese

method

1 Break off the stems of the artichokes and cut off about 2.5 cm/1 inch of the tops, depending on how young and small they are. Remove and discard any coarse outer leaves, leaving only the pale, tender inner leaves. Using a teaspoon, scoop out the chokes. Rub each artichoke with lemon juice as soon as it is prepared, to prevent it from discoloration.

2 Thinly slice the artichokes and place in a salad bowl. Add the rocket, remaining lemon juice and olive oil, season to taste with salt and pepper, and toss well.

3 Using a swivel-bladed vegetable peeler, thinly shave the pecorino over the salad, then serve immediately.

meat &
poultry

Traditionally, wealthy Italians ate the best cuts of meat – often steak and veal – from animals raised on lush pastures, while their less well-off fellow countrymen tenderized the poorer cuts by long, slow cooking, resulting, as is so often the way, in some of the tastiest national dishes.

Veal is still very popular in Italy, and pork, lamb, beef and poultry are also used in many different recipes. This chapter illustrates just a few of the ways in which meat can be used to bring a taste of Italy to your dining table – roasted, grilled, casseroled, pan-fried, combined with tomatoes and seasonings to make a thick, rich sauce for pasta dishes, or with the uniquely creamy-textured Italian rice to make risotto.

Many rural Italian families rear a pig each year for its meat, and any part that is not used for roasts, casseroles, stews, ham and bacon is preserved as one of the many salamis, cured meats and sausages for which Italy is famous. It is worth seeking out the appropriate type of Italian cured meat to use in a recipe – for  example, pancetta, made from salted and spiced belly of pork, adds depth of flavour to Spaghetti alla Carbonara, a light pasta dish with a cream sauce, while luganega, a long, coiled pork sausage from northern Italy, works well with beans in a casserole.

spaghetti with meatballs

ingredients

SERVES 6

1 potato, diced

salt and pepper

400 g/14 oz steak mince

1 onion, finely chopped

1 egg

4 tbsp chopped fresh flat-leaf
    parsley

plain flour, for dusting

5 tbsp virgin olive oil

14 fl oz/400 ml passata

2 tbsp tomato purée

400 g/14 oz dried spaghetti

6 fresh basil leaves, shredded

freshly grated Parmesan
    cheese, to garnish

method

1 Place the potato in a small saucepan, add cold water to cover and a pinch of salt, and bring to the boil. Cook for 10–15 minutes, until tender, then drain. Either mash thoroughly with a potato masher or fork or pass through a potato ricer.

2 Combine the potato, steak, onion, egg and parsley in a bowl and season to taste with salt and pepper. Spread out the flour on a plate. With dampened hands, shape the meat mixture into walnut-size balls and roll in the flour. Shake off any excess.

3 Heat the oil in a heavy-based frying pan, add the meatballs and cook over a medium heat, stirring and turning frequently, for 8–10 minutes, until golden all over.

4 Add the passata and tomato purée and cook for a further 10 minutes, until the sauce is reduced and thickened.

5 Meanwhile, bring a large saucepan of lightly salted water to the boil. Add the pasta, bring back to the boil and cook for 8–10 minutes, until tender but still firm to the bite.

6 Drain well and add to the meatball sauce, tossing well to coat. Transfer to a warmed serving dish, garnish with the basil leaves and Parmesan and serve immediately.

spaghetti bolognese

ingredients

SERVES 4

2 tbsp olive oil

1 tbsp butter

1 small onion, finely chopped

1 carrot, finely chopped

1 celery stick, finely chopped

50 g/1³/4 oz mushrooms, diced

225 g/8 oz beef mince

75 g/2³/4 oz unsmoked bacon
    or ham, diced

2 chicken livers, chopped

2 tbsp tomato purée

125 ml/4 fl oz dry white wine

salt and pepper

¹/2 tsp freshly grated nutmeg

300 ml/10 fl oz chicken stock

125 ml/4 fl oz double cream

450 g/1 lb dried spaghetti

2 tbsp chopped fresh
    flat-leaf parsley, to garnish

freshly grated Parmesan
    cheese, to serve

method

1 Heat the olive oil and butter in a large saucepan over a medium heat. Add the onion, carrot, celery and mushrooms to the pan, then cook until soft. Add the beef and bacon and cook until the beef is evenly browned.

2 Stir in the chicken livers and tomato purée and cook for 2–3 minutes. Pour in the wine and season with salt, pepper and the nutmeg. Add the stock. Bring to the boil, then cover and simmer gently over a low heat for 1 hour. Stir in the cream and simmer, uncovered, until reduced.

3 Bring a large saucepan of lightly salted water to the boil. Add the pasta, return to the boil and cook until tender but still firm to the bite. Drain and transfer to a warmed serving dish.

4 Spoon the meat sauce over the pasta, garnish with the parsley and serve with the Parmesan cheese.

tagliatelle with a rich meat sauce

ingredients

SERVES 4

4 tbsp olive oil, plus extra
　　for drizzling
85 g/3 oz pancetta or rindless
　　lean bacon, diced
1 onion, chopped
1 garlic clove, finely chopped
1 carrot, chopped
1 celery stick, chopped
225 g/8 oz steak mince
8 oz/225 g chicken livers,
　　chopped
2 tbsp passata
125 ml/4 fl oz dry white wine
225 ml/8 fl oz beef stock or
　　water
1 tbsp chopped fresh oregano
1 bay leaf
salt and pepper
450 g/1 lb dried tagliatelle
freshly grated Parmesan
　　cheese, to serve

method

1 Heat the olive oil in a large heavy-based saucepan. Add the pancetta or bacon and cook over a medium heat, stirring occasionally, for 3–5 minutes, until it is just turning brown. Add the onion, garlic, carrot and celery and cook, stirring occasionally, for a further 5 minutes.

2 Add the steak and cook over a high heat, breaking up the meat with a wooden spoon, for 5 minutes, until browned. Stir in the chicken livers and cook, stirring occasionally, for 2–3 minutes. Add the passata, wine, stock, oregano and bay leaf, and season to taste with salt and pepper. Bring to the boil, reduce the heat, cover and simmer for 30–35 minutes.

3 When the sauce is almost cooked, bring a large saucepan of lightly salted water to the boil. Add the pasta, bring back to the boil and cook for 8–10 minutes, until tender but still firm to the bite. Drain, transfer to a warmed serving dish, drizzle with a little olive oil and toss well.

4 Remove and discard the bay leaf from the sauce, then pour the sauce over the pasta, toss again and serve immediately with the grated Parmesan.

grilled steak with tomatoes & garlic

ingredients

SERVES 4

3 tbsp olive oil, plus extra
    for brushing

700 g/1 lb 9 oz tomatoes,
    peeled and chopped

1 red pepper, deseeded
    and chopped

1 onion, chopped

2 garlic cloves, finely
    chopped

1 tbsp chopped fresh flat-leaf
    parsley

1 tsp dried oregano

1 tsp sugar

salt and pepper

4 x 175-g/6-oz entrecôte or
    rump steaks

method

1 Place the oil, tomatoes, red pepper, onion, garlic, parsley, oregano and sugar in a heavy-based saucepan and season to taste with salt and pepper. Bring to the boil, reduce the heat and simmer for 15 minutes.

2 Meanwhile, trim any fat around the outsides of the steaks. Season each generously with pepper (but no salt) and brush with olive oil. Cook under a preheated grill according to taste: 2–3 minutes each side for rare; 3–4 minutes each side for medium and 4–5 minutes on each side for well done.

3 Transfer the steaks to warmed individual plates and spoon the sauce over them. Serve immediately.

beef in red wine

ingredients

SERVES 4

1.25 kg/2 lb 12 oz beef top
    round
salt and pepper
3 tbsp olive oil
1 red onion, chopped
1 garlic clove, finely chopped
2 carrots, sliced
2 celery sticks, sliced
300 ml/10 fl oz Chianti
200 g/7 oz canned tomatoes,
    chopped
1 tbsp chopped fresh oregano
1 tbsp chopped fresh flat-leaf
    parsley
1 bay leaf

method

1 Season the beef all over with salt and pepper.
Heat the olive oil in a large flameproof casserole.
Add the beef and cook over a medium heat,
turning frequently, until browned on all sides.
Use 2 large forks to remove the beef from the
casserole.

2 Reduce the heat, add the onion, garlic, carrots
and celery and cook, stirring occasionally, for
5 minutes, until softened. Pour in the wine
and add the tomatoes, oregano, parsley and
bay leaf. Stir well to mix and bring to the boil.

3 Return the meat to the casserole and
spoon the vegetable mixture over it. Cover
and cook in a preheated oven, 180°C/350°F/
Gas Mark 4, spooning the vegetables over the
meat occasionally, for 3–3¹/₄ hours, until the
beef is tender.

4 Transfer the beef to a carving board and
cover with foil. Place the casserole over a high
heat and bring the juices to the boil. Continue
to boil until reduced and thickened.

5 Carve the beef into slices and place on a
warmed serving platter. Strain the thickened
cooking juices over the beef and serve
immediately.

baked lasagne

ingredients

SERVES 4

meat sauce

3 tbsp olive oil

1 onion, finely chopped

1 celery stick, finely chopped

1 carrot, finely chopped

100 g/3^1/$_2$ oz pancetta, finely
   chopped

175 g/6 oz beef mince

175 g/6 oz pork mince

100 ml/3^1/$_2$ fl oz dry red wine

150 ml/5 fl oz beef stock

1 tbsp tomato purée

salt and pepper

1 clove

1 bay leaf

150 ml/5 fl oz boiling milk

400 g/14 oz dried no-cook
   lasagne verdi

1 quantity Béchamel Sauce
   (see page 174)

150 g/5^1/$_2$ oz mozzarella
   cheese

150 g/5^1/$_2$ oz freshly grated
   Parmesan cheese

55 g/2 oz unsalted butter,
   diced, plus extra for
   greasing

method

1 First, make the meat sauce. Heat the olive oil in a large heavy-based saucepan. Add the onion, celery, carrot, pancetta, beef and pork and cook over a medium heat, stirring frequently and breaking up the meat with a wooden spoon, for 10 minutes, until lightly browned.

2 Add the wine, bring to the boil and cook until reduced. Add about two thirds of the stock, bring to the boil and cook until reduced. Combine the remaining stock and tomato purée and add to the pan. Season to taste, add the clove and bay leaf and pour in the milk. Cover and simmer over a low heat for 1^1/$_2$ hours.

3 Remove the meat sauce from the heat and discard the clove and bay leaf. Lightly grease a large ovenproof dish with butter. Place a layer of the lasagne verdi in the base and cover it with a layer of meat sauce. Spoon a layer of béchamel sauce on top and sprinkle with one third of the mozzarella and Parmesan cheeses. Continue making layers until all the ingredients are used, ending with a topping of béchamel sauce and sprinkled cheese.

5 Dot the top of the lasagne with the diced butter and bake in a preheated oven, 200°C/ 400°F/Gas Mark 6, for 30 minutes, until golden and bubbling.

meatball surprise

ingredients

SERVES 8

500 g/1 lb 2 oz steak mince
500 g/1 lb 2 oz pork mince
2 garlic cloves, finely
    chopped
55 g/2 oz fresh breadcrumbs
50 g/1³/₄ oz freshly grated
    Parmesan cheese
1 tsp dried oregano
¹/₂ tsp ground cinnamon
grated rind and juice of
    1 lemon
2 eggs, lightly beaten
salt and pepper
150 g/5¹/₂ oz fontina cheese
6 tbsp virgin olive oil
140 g/5 oz dried, uncoloured
    breadcrumbs
fresh flat-leaf parsley sprigs,
    to garnish
tomato sauce (see page 80),
    to serve

method

1 Combine the steak, pork, garlic, fresh breadcrumbs, Parmesan, oregano, cinnamon and lemon rind in a bowl. Stir in the lemon juice and beaten eggs, season with salt and pepper and mix well.

2 Knead the mixture with dampened hands, then shape into 16 balls.

3 Cut the fontina into 16 cubes and press 1 cube into each meatball, then reshape them to enclose the cheese completely.

4 Heat the olive oil in a large heavy-based frying pan. Meanwhile, spread out the dried breadcrumbs on a shallow plate and roll the meatballs in them to coat.

5 Add the meatballs, in batches, to the frying pan and cook until golden brown all over. Transfer to an ovenproof dish using a slotted spoon and bake in a preheated oven, 180°C/350°F/Gas Mark 4, for 15–20 minutes, until cooked through. Serve immediately, garnished with parsley sprigs and accompanied by tomato sauce.

pan-fried pork
with mozzarella

ingredients

SERVES 4

450 g/1 lb loin of pork

2–3 garlic cloves, finely
    chopped

175 g/6 oz buffalo mozzarella,
    drained

salt and pepper

12 slices prosciutto

12 fresh sage leaves

55 g/2 oz unsalted butter

flat-leaf parsley sprigs

lemon slices, to garnish

mostarda di Verona, to serve

method

1 Trim any excess fat from the meat, then slice
it crossways into 12 pieces, each about 2.5 cm/
1 inch thick. Beat each slice with the flat end
of a meat mallet or the side of a rolling pin
until thoroughly flattened. Rub each piece all
over with garlic, transfer to a plate and cover
with clingfilm. Set aside in a cool place for
30 minutes to 1 hour.

2 Cut the mozzarella into 12 slices. Season the
pork to taste with salt and pepper, then place
a slice of cheese on top of each slice of pork.
Top with a slice of prosciutto, letting it fall in
folds. Place a sage leaf on each portion and
secure with a cocktail stick.

3 Melt the butter in a large heavy-based frying
pan. Add the pork, in batches if necessary,
and cook for 2–3 minutes on each side, until
the meat is tender and the cheese has melted.
Remove with a slotted spoon and keep warm
while you cook the remaining pork.

4 Remove and discard the cocktail sticks.
Transfer the pork to 4 warmed individual
plates, garnish with parsley sprigs and lemon
slices, and serve immediately with mostarda
di Verona.

pork fillets with fennel

ingredients

SERVES 4

450 g/1 lb pork fillet

2–3 tbsp virgin olive oil

2 tbsp sambuca

1 large fennel bulb, sliced,
    fronds reserved

85 g/3 oz Gorgonzola cheese,
    crumbled

2 tbsp single cream

1 tbsp chopped fresh sage

1 tbsp chopped fresh thyme

salt and pepper

method

1 Trim any fat from the pork and cut into
5-mm/1/4-inch-thick slices. Place the slices
between 2 sheets of clingfilm and beat with
the flat end of a meat mallet or with a rolling pin
to flatten slightly.

2 Heat 2 tablespoons of the oil in a heavy-
based frying pan and add the pork, in batches.
Cook over a medium heat for 2–3 minutes on
each side, until tender. Remove from the pan
and keep warm. Cook the remaining batches,
adding more oil if necessary.

3 Stir the sambuca into the frying pan, increase
the heat and cook, stirring constantly and
scraping up the glazed bits from the bottom.
Add the fennel and cook, stirring and turning
frequently, for 3 minutes. Remove from the
pan and keep warm.

4 Reduce the heat, add the Gorgonzola and
cream and cook, stirring constantly, until
smooth. Remove the pan from the heat, stir
in the sage and thyme and season to taste
with salt and pepper.

5 Divide the pork and fennel between
4 warmed individual serving plates and pour
over the sauce. Garnish with the reserved
fennel fronds and serve immediately.

pork & pasta bake

ingredients

SERVES 4

2 tbsp olive oil

1 onion, chopped

1 garlic clove, finely chopped

2 carrots, diced

55 g/2 oz pancetta, chopped

115 g/4 oz mushrooms,
    chopped

450 g/1 lb pork mince

125 ml/4 fl oz dry white wine

4 tbsp strained canned
    tomatoes

200 g/7 oz canned chopped
    tomatoes

2 tsp chopped fresh sage

salt and pepper

225 g/8 oz dried elicoidali

140 g/5 oz mozzarella
    cheese, diced

4 tbsp freshly grated
    Parmesan cheese

300 ml/10 fl oz hot Béchamel
    Sauce (see page 174)

method

1 Heat the olive oil in a large heavy-based frying pan. Add the onion, garlic and carrots and cook over a low heat, stirring occasionally, for 5 minutes, or until the onion has softened. Add the pancetta and cook for 5 minutes. Add the chopped mushrooms and cook, stirring occasionally, for a further 2 minutes. Add the pork and cook, breaking it up with a wooden spoon, until the meat is browned all over. Stir in the wine, strained tomatoes, chopped tomatoes and their can juices, and sage. Season to taste with salt and pepper and bring to the boil, then cover and simmer over a low heat for 25–30 minutes.

2 Meanwhile, bring a large heavy-based saucepan of lightly salted water to the boil. Add the pasta, return to the boil and cook for 8–10 minutes, or until tender but still firm to the bite.

3 Spoon the pork mixture into a large ovenproof dish. Stir the mozzarella and half the Parmesan cheese into the béchamel sauce. Drain the pasta and stir the sauce into it, then spoon it over the pork mixture. Sprinkle with the remaining Parmesan cheese and bake in a preheated oven, 200°C/400°F/ Gas Mark 6, for 25–30 minutes, or until golden brown. Serve immediately.

spicy pork risotto

ingredients

SERVES 4

1 thick slice white bread,
    crust removed and
    discarded, soaked in water
    or milk for 5 minutes

450 g/1 lb pork mince

2 garlic cloves, minced

1 tbsp finely chopped onion

1 tsp black peppercorns,
    lightly crushed

salt and pepper

1 egg

corn oil, for pan-frying

400 g/14 oz canned chopped
    tomatoes

1 tbsp tomato purée

1 tsp dried oregano

1 tsp fennel seeds

pinch of sugar

3 tbsp butter

1 tbsp olive oil

1 small onion, finely chopped

280 g/10 oz risotto rice

150 ml/5 fl oz red wine

1 litre/1³/4 pints simmering
    beef stock

fresh basil leaves, to garnish

method

1 Drain the bread and squeeze to remove all the liquid. Mix the bread, pork, garlic, onion, crushed peppercorns and a pinch of salt together in a bowl. Add the egg and mix well.

2 Heat the corn oil in a frying pan over a medium heat. Form the meat mixture into balls and cook a few at a time until browned. Remove each batch from the pan and drain.

3 Combine the tomatoes, tomato purée, oregano, fennel seeds and sugar in a heavy-based saucepan. Add the meatballs. Bring the sauce to the boil over a medium heat, then reduce the heat and simmer for 30 minutes.

4 Melt 2 tablespoons of the butter with the olive oil in a deep saucepan over a medium heat. Stir in the onion and cook, stirring frequently, for 5 minutes, until soft.

5 Reduce the heat and stir in the rice. Cook, stirring, for 2–3 minutes, or until the grains are translucent. Add the wine and cook, stirring, for 1 minute until reduced. Gradually add the hot stock, a ladleful at a time, stirring constantly until the liquid is absorbed. Continue stirring in the stock until all the liquid is absorbed and the rice is creamy. Season to taste.

6 Lift out the cooked meatballs and add to the risotto. Remove from the heat and stir in the remaining butter. Serve the risotto and meatballs drizzled with tomato sauce. Garnish with basil.

cannelloni with spinach & ricotta

ingredients

SERVES 4

12 dried cannelloni tubes,
7.5-cm/3-inch long

butter, for greasing

filling

140 g/5 oz lean ham,
chopped

140 g/5 oz frozen spinach,
thawed and drained

115 g/4 oz ricotta cheese

1 egg

3 tbsp freshly grated pecorino
cheese

pinch of freshly grated
nutmeg

salt and pepper

cheese sauce

600 ml/1 pint milk

25 g/1 oz unsalted butter

2 tbsp plain flour

85 g/3 oz freshly grated
Gruyère cheese

salt and pepper

method

1 Bring a large saucepan of lightly salted water to the boil. Add the cannelloni tubes, bring back to the boil, and cook for 6–7 minutes, until nearly tender. Drain and rinse under cold water, then spread out on a clean tea towel.

2 Put the ham, spinach and ricotta in a food processor and process for a few seconds until combined. Add the egg and pecorino and process to a smooth paste. Transfer the filling to a bowl, add the nutmeg and season to taste.

3 Spoon the filling into a pastry bag fitted with a 1-cm/1/2-inch nozzle. Carefully open one cannelloni tube, stand it upright, and pipe in the filling. Place in an ovenproof dish greased with butter and fill the remaining cannelloni.

4 To make the cheese sauce, heat the milk to just below boiling point. Melt the butter in another saucepan. Stir in the flour and cook over a low heat, stirring constantly, for 1 minute. Gradually stir in the hot milk, then bring to the boil, stirring constantly. Simmer over a very low heat, stirring frequently, for 10 minutes, until thick and smooth. Remove the pan from the heat, stir in the Gruyère and season to taste.

5 Spoon the sauce over the filled cannelloni. Bake in a preheated oven, 180°C/350°F/Gas Mark 4, for 20–25 minutes. Serve immediately.

spaghetti alla carbonara

ingredients

SERVES 4

450 g/1 lb dried spaghetti

1 tbsp olive oil

225 g/8 oz rindless pancetta
    or lean bacon, chopped

4 eggs

5 tbsp single cream

salt and pepper

4 tbsp freshly grated
    Parmesan cheese

method

1 Bring a large heavy-based saucepan of lightly salted water to the boil. Add the pasta, return to the boil and cook for 8–10 minutes, or until tender but still firm to the bite.

2 Meanwhile, heat the olive oil in a heavy-based frying pan. Add the chopped pancetta and cook over a medium heat, stirring frequently, for 8–10 minutes.

3 Beat the eggs with the cream in a small bowl and season to taste with salt and pepper. Drain the pasta and return it to the pan. Tip in the contents of the frying pan, then add the egg mixture and half the Parmesan cheese. Stir well, then transfer to a warmed serving dish. Serve immediately, sprinkled with the remaining Parmesan cheese.

sausages with borlotti beans

ingredients

SERVES 4

2 tbsp virgin olive oil

500 g/1 lb 2 oz luganega or
other Italian sausage

140 g/5 oz smoked pancetta
or lean bacon, diced

2 red onions, chopped

2 garlic cloves, finely
chopped

225 g/8 oz dried borlotti
beans, covered and
soaked overnight in cold
water

2 tsp finely chopped fresh
rosemary

2 tsp chopped fresh sage

300 ml/10 fl oz dry white wine

salt and pepper

fresh rosemary sprigs,
to garnish

crusty bread, to serve

method

1 Heat the oil in a flameproof casserole. Add the sausages and cook over a low heat, turning frequently, for 10 minutes, or until browned all over. Remove from the casserole and set aside.

2 Add the pancetta to the casserole, increase the heat to medium and cook, stirring frequently, for 5 minutes, or until golden brown. Remove with a slotted spoon and set aside.

3 Add the onions to the casserole and cook over a low heat, stirring occasionally, for 5 minutes, until softened. Add the garlic and cook for a further 2 minutes.

4 Drain the beans and set aside the soaking liquid. Add the beans to the casserole, then return the sausages and pancetta. Gently stir in the herbs and pour in the wine. Measure the reserved soaking liquid and add 300 ml/ 10 fl oz to the casserole. Season to taste with salt and pepper. Bring to the boil over a low heat and boil for 15 minutes, then transfer to a preheated oven, 140°C/275°F/Gas Mark 1, and cook for 2$\frac{3}{4}$ hours.

5 Remove the casserole from the oven and ladle the sausages and beans onto 4 warmed plates. Garnish with the rosemary sprigs and serve immediately with crusty bread.

sausage & rosemary risotto

ingredients

SERVES 4–6

2 long fresh rosemary sprigs,
plus extra to garnish
2 tbsp olive oil
55 g/2 oz butter
1 large onion, finely chopped
1 celery stick, finely chopped
2 garlic cloves, finely
chopped
$^1/_2$ tsp dried thyme leaves
450 g/1 lb pork sausage,
such as luganega or
cumberland, cut into
1-cm/$^1/_2$-inch pieces
350 g/12 oz risotto rice
125 ml/4 fl oz fruity red wine
1.3 litres/2$^1/_4$ pints simmering
chicken stock
salt and pepper
85 g/3 oz freshly grated
Parmesan cheese

method

1 Strip the long thin leaves from the rosemary sprigs and chop finely, then set aside.

2 Heat the oil and half the butter in a deep saucepan over a medium heat. Add the onion and celery and cook, stirring occasionally, for 2 minutes. Stir in the garlic, thyme, sausage and rosemary. Cook, stirring frequently, for 5 minutes, or until the sausage starts to brown. Transfer the sausage to a plate.

3 Reduce the heat and stir in the rice. Cook, stirring constantly, for 2–3 minutes, or until the grains are translucent.

4 Add the wine and cook, stirring, for 1 minute until reduced. Gradually add the hot stock, a ladleful at a time. Stir constantly and add more liquid as the rice absorbs each addition. Increase the heat to medium so that the liquid bubbles. Cook for 20 minutes, or until all the liquid is absorbed and the rice is creamy.

5 Toward the end of cooking, return the sausage pieces to the risotto and heat through. Season to taste. Remove from the heat and add the remaining butter. Mix well, then stir in the Parmesan until it melts. Spoon the risotto onto warmed plates, garnish with rosemary sprigs and serve.

pepperoni pasta

ingredients

SERVES 4

3 tbsp olive oil

1 onion, chopped

1 red pepper, deseeded and diced

1 orange pepper, deseeded and diced

800 g/1 lb 12 oz canned chopped tomatoes

1 tbsp sun-dried tomato purée

1 tsp paprika

225 g/8 oz pepperoni, sliced

2 tbsp chopped fresh flat-leaf parsley, plus extra to garnish

salt and pepper

450 g/1 lb dried garganelli

mixed salad leaves, to serve

method

1 Heat 2 tablespoons of the olive oil in a large heavy-based frying pan. Add the onion and cook over a low heat, stirring occasionally, for 5 minutes, or until softened. Add the red and orange peppers, tomatoes and their can juices, sun-dried tomato purée and paprika to the pan and bring to the boil.

2 Add the pepperoni and parsley and season to taste with salt and pepper. Stir well and bring to the boil, then reduce the heat and simmer for 10–15 minutes.

3 Meanwhile, bring a large heavy-based saucepan of lightly salted water to the boil. Add the pasta, return to the boil, and cook for 8–10 minutes, or until tender but still firm to the bite. Drain well and transfer to a warmed serving dish. Add the remaining olive oil and toss. Add the sauce and toss again. Sprinkle with parsley and serve immediately with mixed salad leaves.

four seasons pizza

ingredients

SERVES 2

pizza dough (see page 200)
plain flour, for dusting
oil, for oiling

tomato sauce

2 tbsp olive oil
1 small onion, finely chopped
1 garlic clove, finely chopped
1 red pepper, deseeded and
    chopped
225 g/8 oz plum tomatoes,
    peeled and chopped
1 tbsp tomato purée
1 tsp soft brown sugar
1 tbsp shredded fresh basil
1 bay leaf
salt and pepper

topping

70 g/2¹/₂ oz cooked prawns
55 g/2 oz bottled artichoke
    hearts, thinly sliced
25 g/1 oz mozzarella cheese,
    drained and thinly sliced
1 tomato, thinly sliced
100 g/3¹/₂ oz mushrooms or
    pepperoni, thinly sliced
2 tsp capers, rinsed
2 tsp stoned, sliced black
    olives
salt and pepper
2 tbsp olive oil

method

1 To make the tomato sauce, heat the olive oil in a heavy-based saucepan. Add the onion, garlic and pepper and cook over a low heat, stirring occasionally, for 5 minutes, until softened. Add the tomatoes, tomato purée, sugar, basil and bay leaf, and season to taste with salt and pepper. Cover and simmer, stirring occasionally, for 30 minutes, until thickened. Remove the pan from the heat and let the sauce cool completely.

2 Turn out the prepared pizza dough onto a lightly floured work surface and knock down. Knead briefly, then cut it in half and roll out each piece into a circle about 5 mm/¹/₄ inch thick. Transfer to a lightly oiled baking sheet and push up the edges with your fingers to form a small rim.

3 Spread the tomato sauce over the pizza bases, almost to the edge. Cover one quarter with prawns. Cover a second quarter with sliced artichoke hearts. Cover the third quarter with alternate slices of mozzarella and tomato. Cover the final quarter with sliced mushrooms. Sprinkle the surface with capers and olives, season to taste with salt and pepper, and drizzle with the olive oil.

4 Bake in a preheated oven, 220°C/425°F/ Gas Mark 7, for 20–25 minutes, until the crust is crisp and the cheese has melted. Serve immediately.

roast lamb with rosemary & marsala

ingredients

SERVES 6

1.8 kg/4 lb leg of lamb
2 garlic cloves, thinly sliced
2 tbsp rosemary leaves
8 tbsp olive oil
salt and pepper
900 g/2 lb potatoes, cut into
  2.5-cm/1-inch cubes
6 fresh sage leaves, chopped
150 ml/5 fl oz Marsala

method

1 Use a small, sharp knife to make incisions all over the lamb, opening them out slightly to make little pockets. Insert the garlic slices and about half the rosemary leaves in the pockets.

2 Place the lamb in a roasting tin and spoon over half the olive oil. Roast in a preheated oven, 220°C/425°F/Gas Mark 7, for 15 minutes. Reduce the oven temperature to 180°C/350°F/Gas Mark 4. Remove the lamb from the oven and season to taste. Turn the lamb over, return to the oven and roast for a further hour.

3 Meanwhile, spread out the cubed potatoes in a second roasting tin, pour the remaining olive oil over them and toss to coat. Sprinkle with the remaining rosemary and the sage. Place the potatoes in the oven with the lamb and roast for 40 minutes.

4 Remove the lamb from the oven, turn it over and pour over the Marsala. Return it to the oven with the potatoes and cook for a further 15 minutes.

5 Transfer the lamb to a carving board and cover with foil. Place the roasting tin over a high heat, bring the juices to the boil and boil until thickened and syrupy. Strain into a warmed gravy boat or jug. Carve the lamb into slices and serve with the potatoes and sauce.

lamb shanks with roasted onions

ingredients

SERVES 4

4 x 350-g/12-oz lamb shanks,
    any excess fat trimmed off
6 garlic cloves, each cut into
    4 slices lengthways
2 tbsp virgin olive oil
1 tbsp very finely chopped
    fresh rosemary
salt and pepper
4 red onions
350 g/12 oz carrots, cut into
    thin sticks
4 tbsp water

method

1 Using a small, sharp knife, make 6 incisions in each lamb shank. Insert a garlic slice in each incision. Place the lamb in a single layer in a roasting pan, drizzle with the olive oil, sprinkle with the rosemary and season with pepper. Roast in a preheated oven, 180°C/350°F/ Gas Mark 4, for 45 minutes.

2 Wrap each onion in a square of foil. Remove the lamb shanks from the oven and season with salt. Return the pan to the oven and place the onions on the shelf next to it. Roast for a further 1 hour, or until the lamb is tender.

3 Bring a large saucepan of water to the boil. Add the carrot sticks and blanch for 1 minute. Drain and refresh under cold water.

4 Remove the roasting tin from the oven and transfer the lamb to a warmed serving dish. Skim off any fat from the roasting tin and place over a medium heat. Add the carrots and cook for 2 minutes, then add the water, bring to the boil and simmer, stirring constantly and scraping up the glazed bits from the bottom of the tin.

5 Transfer the carrots and sauce to the serving dish. Remove the onions from the oven and unwrap. Cut off and discard about 1 cm/ 1/2 inch of the tops of the onions and add the onions to the dish. Serve immediately.

spicy lamb with black olives

ingredients

SERVES 6

6 tbsp olive oil

1 onion, chopped

2 garlic cloves, finely
    chopped

1.25 kg/2 lb 12 oz boneless
    leg of lamb, cut into
    2.5-cm/1-inch cubes

2 dried whole peperoncini or
    other red chillies

175 ml/6 fl oz dry white wine

175 g/6 oz black olives,
    stoned

2 tbsp chopped fresh flat-leaf
    parsley, plus extra
    to garnish

salt

method

1 Heat the olive oil in a large flameproof casserole. Add the onion and garlic and cook over a low heat, stirring occasionally, for 5 minutes, until softened.

2 Add the cubed lamb and cook, stirring frequently, for 5 minutes, until browned all over. Crumble in the chillies, pour in the wine and cook for a further 5 minutes. Stir in the olives and parsley and season to taste with salt.

3 Transfer the casserole to a preheated oven, 180°C/350°F/Gas Mark 4, and cook for 1 1/2 hours, until the lamb is tender. Garnish with extra parsley and serve immediately.

hot pepper lamb in red wine risotto

ingredients

SERVES 4

4 tbsp plain flour, seasoned
  with salt and pepper

8 pieces neck of lamb

4 tbsp olive oil

1 green pepper, deseeded
  and thinly sliced

1–2 fresh green chillies,
  deseeded and thinly sliced

2 small onions, 1 thinly
  sliced, 1 finely chopped

2 garlic cloves, thinly sliced

2 tbsp torn fresh basil

125 ml/4 fl oz red wine

4 tbsp red wine vinegar

8 cherry tomatoes

125 ml/4 fl oz water

3 tbsp butter

280 g/10 oz risotto rice

125 ml/4 fl oz simmering
  chicken stock

salt and pepper

85 g/3 oz freshly grated
  Parmesan cheese

method

1 Spread the flour on a plate and coat the lamb, shaking off any excess. Heat 3 tablespoons of the oil in a large casserole over a high heat. Add the lamb and cook until browned. Remove from the casserole and set aside.

2 Lightly brown the pepper, chillies, sliced onion, garlic and basil in the casserole. Add the wine and vinegar, bring to the boil and cook over a high heat for 3–4 minutes until the liquid is reduced to 2 tablespoons. Stir in the tomatoes and water and bring to the boil. Add the meat, cover, and reduce the heat to low. Cook for 30 minutes until the meat is tender.

3 Melt 2 tablespoons of the butter with the remaining oil in a deep saucepan over a medium heat. Add the chopped onion and cook, stirring occasionally, for 5 minutes, until soft. Reduce the heat and stir in the rice. Cook, stirring, for 2–3 minutes, or until the grains are translucent.

4 Gradually add the hot stock, a ladleful at a time, stirring constantly until the liquid is absorbed. Continue stirring in the stock until all the liquid is absorbed and the rice is creamy. Season to taste.

5 Remove the risotto from the heat. Stir in the remaining butter and the Parmesan and serve, topped with the lamb.

veal with prosciutto & sage

ingredients

SERVES 4

4 veal escalopes
2 tbsp lemon juice
salt and pepper
1 tbsp chopped fresh
    sage leaves
4 slices prosciutto
55 g/2 oz unsalted butter
3 tbsp dry white wine

method

1 Place the veal escalopes between 2 sheets of clingfilm and pound with the flat end of a meat mallet or the side of a rolling pin until very thin. Transfer to a plate and sprinkle with the lemon juice. Set aside for 30 minutes, spooning the juice over them occasionally.

2 Pat the escalopes dry with kitchen paper, season with salt and pepper and rub with half the sage. Place a slice of prosciutto on each scallop and secure with a cocktail stick.

3 Melt the butter in a large heavy-based frying pan. Add the remaining sage and cook over a low heat, stirring constantly, for 1 minute. Add the escalopes and cook for 3–4 minutes on each side, until golden brown. Pour in the wine and cook for a further 2 minutes.

4 Transfer the escalopes to a warmed serving dish and pour the pan juices over them. Remove and discard the cocktail sticks and serve immediately.

milanese veal

ingredients

SERVES 4

1 tbsp virgin olive oil
4 tbsp butter
2 onions, chopped
1 leek, chopped
3 tbsp plain flour
salt and pepper
4 thick slices of veal shin
    (osso bucco)
300 ml/10 fl oz white wine
300 ml/10 fl oz veal or
    chicken stock

gremolata

2 tbsp chopped fresh parsley
1 garlic clove, finely chopped
grated rind of 1 lemon

method

1 Heat the oil and butter in a large heavy-based frying pan. Add the onions and leek and cook over a low heat, stirring occasionally, for 5 minutes, until softened.

2 Spread out the flour on a plate and season with salt and pepper. Toss the pieces of veal in the flour to coat, shaking off any excess. Add the veal to the frying pan, increase the heat to high and cook until browned on both sides.

3 Gradually stir in the wine and stock and bring just to the boil, stirring constantly. Reduce the heat, cover and simmer for 1 1/4 hours, or until the veal is very tender.

4 Meanwhile, make the gremolata by mixing the parsley, garlic and lemon rind in a small bowl.

5 Transfer the veal to a warmed serving dish with a slotted spoon. Bring the sauce to the boil and cook, stirring occasionally, until thickened and reduced. Pour the sauce over the veal, sprinkle with the gremolata and serve immediately.

tuscan chicken

ingredients

SERVES 4

2 tbsp plain flour

salt and pepper

4 skinned chicken quarters
   or portions

3 tbsp olive oil

1 red onion, chopped

2 garlic cloves, finely
   chopped

1 red pepper, deseeded
   and chopped

pinch of saffron threads

150 ml/5 fl oz chicken stock
   or a mixture of chicken
   stock and dry white wine

400 g/14 oz canned
   tomatoes, chopped

4 sun-dried tomatoes in oil,
   drained and chopped

225 g/8 oz portobello
   mushrooms, sliced

115 g/4 oz black olives,
   stoned

4 tbsp lemon juice

fresh basil leaves, to garnish

method

1 Place the flour on a shallow plate and season with salt and pepper. Coat the chicken in the seasoned flour, shaking off any excess. Heat the olive oil in a large flameproof casserole. Add the chicken and cook over a medium heat, turning frequently, for 5–7 minutes, until golden brown. Remove from the casserole and set aside.

2 Add the onion, garlic and red pepper to the casserole, reduce the heat and cook, stirring occasionally, for 5 minutes, until softened. Meanwhile, stir the saffron into the stock.

3 Stir the tomatoes and their can juices, the sun-dried tomatoes, mushrooms and olives into the casserole and cook, stirring occasionally, for 3 minutes. Pour in the stock and saffron mixture and the lemon juice. Bring to the boil, then return the chicken to the casserole.

4 Cover and cook in a preheated oven, 180°C/350°F/Gas Mark 4, for 1 hour, until the chicken is tender. Garnish with the basil leaves and serve immediately.

pappardelle with chicken & porcini

ingredients

SERVES 4

40 g/1¹/₂ oz dried porcini
    mushrooms

175 ml/6 fl oz hot water

800 g/1 lb 12 oz canned
    chopped tomatoes

1 fresh red chilli, deseeded
    and finely chopped

3 tbsp olive oil

350 g/12 oz skinless,
    boneless chicken, cut into
    thin strips

2 garlic cloves, finely
    chopped

350 g/12 oz dried
    pappardelle

salt and pepper

2 tbsp chopped fresh flat-leaf
    parsley, to garnish

method

1 Place the porcini in a small bowl, add the hot water and soak for 30 minutes. Meanwhile, place the tomatoes and their can juices in a heavy-based saucepan and break them up with a wooden spoon, then stir in the chilli. Bring to the boil, then reduce the heat and simmer, stirring occasionally, for 30 minutes, or until reduced.

2 Remove the mushrooms from their soaking liquid with a slotted spoon, reserving the liquid. Strain the liquid through a muslin-lined sieve into the tomatoes and simmer for a further 15 minutes. Meanwhile, heat 2 tablespoons of the olive oil in a heavy-based frying pan. Add the chicken and cook, stirring frequently, until golden brown all over and tender. Stir in the mushrooms and garlic and cook for a further 5 minutes.

3 While the chicken is cooking, bring a large heavy-based saucepan of lightly salted water to the boil. Add the pasta, return to the boil and cook for 8–10 minutes, or until tender but still firm to the bite. Drain well, then transfer to a warmed serving dish. Drizzle the pasta with the remaining olive oil and toss lightly. Stir the chicken mixture into the tomato sauce, season to taste and spoon onto the pasta. Toss lightly, sprinkle with parsley and serve immediately.

creamy chicken ravioli

ingredients

SERVES 4

115 g/4 oz cooked skinless,
    boneless chicken breast,
    roughly chopped
55 g/2 oz cooked spinach
55 g/2 oz prosciutto, roughly
    chopped
1 shallot, roughly chopped
4 tbsp freshly grated pecorino
    cheese
pinch of freshly grated
    nutmeg
2 eggs, lightly beaten
salt and pepper
1 quantity basic pasta dough
    (see page 164, omitting
    spinach from the recipe)
plain flour, for dusting
fresh basil sprigs, to garnish

sauce

300 ml/10 fl oz double cream
    or panna da cucina
2 garlic cloves, finely
    chopped
115 g/4 oz chestnut
    mushrooms, thinly sliced
2 tbsp freshly grated pecorino
    cheese
salt and pepper
2 tbsp shredded fresh basil

method

1 Place the chicken, spinach, prosciutto and shallot in a food processor and process until chopped and blended. Transfer to a bowl and stir in 2 tablespoons of the pecorino cheese, the nutmeg and half the egg. Season to taste.

2 Halve the pasta dough. Wrap one piece in clingfilm and thinly roll out the other on a lightly floured work surface. Cover with a tea towel and roll out the second piece of dough. Place small mounds of the filling in rows 4 cm/ 1^1/2 inches apart on one sheet of dough and brush the spaces in between with beaten egg. Fit the second piece of dough on top. Press down firmly between the mounds of filling, pushing out any air. Cut into squares, place on a floured tea towel and let rest for 1 hour.

3 Bring a large saucepan of lightly salted water to the boil. Add the ravioli, in batches, return to the boil and cook for 5 minutes. Remove with a slotted spoon and drain on kitchen paper, then transfer to a warmed dish.

4 Meanwhile, to make the sauce, pour the cream into a frying pan, add the garlic and bring to the boil. Simmer for 1 minute, then add the mushrooms and the cheese. Season to taste and simmer for 3 minutes. Stir in the basil, then pour the sauce over the ravioli. Serve sprinkled with the remaining cheese, garnished with basil sprigs.

chicken tortellini

ingredients

SERVES 4

115 g/4 oz boned chicken
    breast, skinned
55 g/2 oz prosciutto
40 g/1^1/$_2$ oz cooked spinach,
    well drained
1 tbsp finely chopped onion
4 tbsp freshly grated
    Parmesan cheese
pinch of ground allspice
1 egg, beaten
salt and pepper
450 g/1 lb basic pasta dough
    (see page 164, omitting
    spinach from the recipe)
2 tbsp chopped fresh parsley,
    to garnish

sauce

300 ml/10 fl oz single cream
2 garlic cloves, crushed
115 g/4 oz white mushrooms,
    thinly sliced
2 tbsp freshly grated
    Parmesan cheese
salt and pepper

method

1 Bring a pan of salted water to the boil. Add the chicken and poach for about 10 minutes. Cool slightly, then place in a food processor with the prosciutto, spinach and onion and process until finely chopped. Stir in half of the Parmesan cheese, allspice and egg and season with salt and pepper to taste.

2 Thinly roll out the pasta dough and cut into 4–5-cm/1^1/$_2$–2-inch circles.

3 Place ^{1}/$_2$ teaspoon of the chicken and ham filling in the centre of each circle. Fold the pieces in half and press the edges to seal, then wrap each piece round your index finger, cross over the ends, and curl the rest of the dough backward to make a navel shape. Re-roll the trimmings and repeat until all of the dough is used up.

4 Bring a saucepan of salted water to the boil. Add the tortellini, in batches, return to the boil and cook for 5 minutes. Drain the tortellini well and transfer to a serving dish.

5 To make the sauce, bring the cream and garlic to the boil in a small saucepan, then simmer for 3 minutes. Add the mushrooms and the cheese, season to taste with salt and pepper and simmer for 2–3 minutes. Pour the sauce over the tortellini. Sprinkle over the remaining Parmesan cheese, garnish with the parsley and serve.

chicken, mushroom & cashew risotto

ingredients

SERVES 4

55 g/2 oz butter

1 onion, chopped

250 g/9 oz skinless, boneless
    chicken breasts, diced

350 g/12 oz risotto rice

1 tsp ground turmeric

150 ml/5 fl oz white wine

1.3 litres/2^1/4 pints simmering
    chicken stock

75 g/2^3/4 oz chestnut
    mushrooms, sliced

50 g/1^3/4 oz cashews, halved

salt and pepper

to garnish

wild rocket

fresh Parmesan
    cheese shavings

fresh basil leaves

method

1 Melt the butter in a large saucepan over a medium heat. Add the onion and cook, stirring occasionally, for 5 minutes, or until softened. Add the chicken and cook, stirring frequently, for a further 5 minutes.

2 Reduce the heat, add the rice and mix to coat in butter. Cook, stirring constantly, for 2–3 minutes, or until the grains are translucent.

3 Stir in the turmeric, then add the wine. Cook, stirring constantly, for 1 minute until reduced.

4 Gradually add the hot stock, a ladleful at a time. Stir constantly and add more liquid as the rice absorbs each addition. Increase the heat to medium so that the liquid bubbles. Cook for 20 minutes, or until all the liquid is absorbed and the rice is creamy.

5 About 3 minutes before the end of the cooking time, stir in the mushrooms and cashews. Season to taste.

6 Arrange the rocket leaves on 4 individual serving plates. Remove the risotto from the heat and spoon it over the rocket. Sprinkle over the Parmesan shavings and basil leaves and serve.

risotto with chargrilled chicken breast

ingredients

SERVES 4

4 boneless chicken breasts, about 115 g/4 oz each, seasoned with salt and pepper

grated rind and juice of 1 lemon

5 tbsp olive oil

1 garlic clove, crushed

8 fresh thyme sprigs, finely chopped

3 tbsp butter

1 small onion, finely chopped

280 g/10 oz risotto rice

150 ml/5 fl oz dry white wine

1 litre/1³/4 pints simmering chicken stock

salt and pepper

85 g/3 oz freshly grated Parmesan or Grana Padano cheese

lemon wedges and fresh thyme sprigs, to garnish

method

1 Place the chicken in a shallow, non-metallic dish. Combine the lemon rind and juice, 4 tablespoons of the olive oil, the garlic and thyme in a bowl and rub into the chicken. Cover and marinate in the refrigerator for 4–6 hours. Return the chicken to room temperature.

2 Preheat a griddle pan over a high heat. Cook the chicken, skin-side down, for 10 minutes, or until the skin is crisp and brown. Turn over and brown the underside. Reduce the heat and cook for a further 10–15 minutes, until the juices run clear. Rest on a carving board for 5 minutes, then cut into slices.

3 Heat 2 tablespoons of the butter with the remaining oil in a deep saucepan over a medium heat. Add the onion and cook, stirring, for 5 minutes, until soft. Reduce the heat and stir in the rice. Cook, stirring, for 2–3 minutes, until the grains are translucent. Add the wine and cook, stirring, for 1 minute.

4 Gradually add the hot stock, a ladleful at a time, stirring constantly until the liquid is absorbed. Continue stirring in the stock until all the liquid is absorbed and the rice is creamy.

5 Remove the risotto from the heat, season to taste and stir in the remaining butter, then the Parmesan. Serve topped with the chicken slices and garnished with lemon and thyme.

fish &
seafood

Almost surrounded by sea, and with its many lakes and rivers, it is not surprising that Italy has a tradition of cooking and eating fine fish. Generations of Italian cooks have perfected the art of preparing and cooking fish and seafood in recipes that bring out their flavour and texture to perfection.

Unfortunately, what was once an inexpensive, or even free, source of food is rapidly becoming a luxury item because marine pollution and over-enthusiastic fishing have resulted in stocks being depleted. However, there are still some species of saltwater fish that are not found elsewhere and are often only available in preserved form. Anchovies, for example, are rarely seen fresh outside the Mediterranean, but the canned or salted versions (rinsed well before use) are useful for adding a distinctive flavour to pasta sauces, pizzas and salads. Tuna is another Mediterranean favourite, a large oily fish that is fabulous cut into fresh steaks, and a very versatile store-cupboard item canned in oil or brine.

Other Italian favourites include swordfish, red mullet, sea bream, sea bass, sardines and shellfish, as well as freshwater fish such as trout. If you are a seafood fan, try cooking your own favourite in the Italian style – delicious and nutritious.

red mullet with capers & olives

ingredients

SERVES 4

700 g/1 lb 9 oz mullet fillets
(about 12)

3 tbsp chopped fresh
marjoram or flat-leaf
parsley

thinly peeled rind of 1 orange,
cut into thin strips

225 g/8 oz mixed salad
leaves, torn into pieces

3 tbsp virgin olive oil

1 fennel bulb, cut into thin
sticks

dressing

175 ml/6 fl oz extra virgin
olive oil

1 tbsp balsamic vinegar

1 tbsp white wine vinegar

1 tsp Dijon mustard

salt and pepper

sauce

1 tbsp butter

40 g/1 1/2 oz black olives,
stoned and thinly sliced

1 tbsp capers, rinsed

method

1 Place the fish fillets on a plate, sprinkle with the marjoram and season to taste. Set aside.

2 Blanch the orange rind in a small saucepan of boiling water for 2 minutes, drain, refresh under cold water and drain well again. Place the mixed salad leaves in a large bowl.

3 To make the dressing, whisk together the extra virgin olive oil, vinegars and mustard in a small bowl and season to taste. Alternatively, shake all the dressing ingredients in a screw-top jar. Pour the dressing over the salad leaves and toss well. Arrange the salad leaves on a large serving platter to make a bed.

4 Heat the virgin olive oil in a large heavy-based frying pan. Add the fennel and cook, stirring constantly, for 1 minute. Remove the fennel with a slotted spoon, set aside and keep warm. Add the fish fillets, skin-side down, and cook for 2 minutes. Carefully turn them over and cook for a further 1–2 minutes. Remove from the pan and drain on kitchen paper. Keep warm.

5 To make the sauce, melt the butter in a small saucepan, add the olives and capers and cook, stirring constantly, for 1 minute.

6 Place the fish fillets on the bed of salad leaves, top with the orange rind and fennel and pour over the sauce. Serve immediately.

roast sea bream with fennel

ingredients

SERVES 4

250 g/9 oz dried, uncoloured
    breadcrumbs

2 tbsp milk

1 fennel bulb, thinly sliced,
    fronds reserved for garnish

1 tbsp lemon juice

2 tbsp sambuca

1 tbsp chopped fresh thyme

1 bay leaf, crumbled

1.5 kg/3 lb 5 oz whole sea
    bream, cleaned, scaled
    and boned

salt and pepper

3 tbsp olive oil, plus extra
    for brushing

1 red onion, chopped

300 ml/10 fl oz dry white wine

method

1 Place the breadcrumbs in a bowl, add the milk and set aside for 5 minutes to soak. Place the fennel in another bowl and add the lemon juice, sambuca, thyme and bay leaf. Squeeze the breadcrumbs and add them to the mixture, stirring well.

2 Rinse the fish inside and out under cold running water and pat dry with kitchen paper. Season with salt and pepper. Spoon the fennel mixture into the cavity, then bind the fish with kitchen string.

3 Brush a large ovenproof dish with olive oil and sprinkle the onion over the bottom. Lay the fish on top and pour in the wine – it should come about one third of the way up the fish. Drizzle the sea bream with the olive oil and cook in preheated oven, 240°C/475°F/ Gas Mark 9, for 25–30 minutes. Baste the fish occasionally with the cooking juices and if it starts to brown, cover with a piece of foil to protect it.

4 Carefully lift out the fish, remove the string and place on a warmed serving platter. Garnish with the reserved fennel fronds and serve immediately.

swordfish with olives & capers

ingredients

SERVES 4

2 tbsp plain flour

salt and pepper

4 x 225-g/8-oz swordfish
    steaks

100 ml/3^1/$_2$ fl oz olive oil

2 garlic cloves, halved

1 onion, chopped

4 anchovy fillets, drained and
    chopped

4 tomatoes, peeled, deseeded
    and chopped

12 green olives, stoned and
    sliced

1 tbsp capers, rinsed

fresh rosemary leaves,
    to garnish

method

1 Spread out the flour on a plate and season with salt and pepper. Coat the fish in the seasoned flour, shaking off any excess.

2 Gently heat the olive oil in a large heavy-based frying pan. Add the garlic and cook over a low heat for 2–3 minutes, until just golden. Do not let it turn brown or burn. Remove the garlic and discard.

3 Add the fish to the pan and cook over a medium heat for about 4 minutes on each side, until cooked through and golden brown. Remove the fish from the pan and set aside.

4 Add the onion and anchovies to the pan and cook, mashing the anchovies with a wooden spoon until they have turned to a purée and the onion is golden. Add the tomatoes and cook over a low heat, stirring occasionally, for about 20 minutes, until the mixture has thickened.

5 Stir in the olives and capers and taste and adjust the seasoning. Return the steaks to the pan and heat through gently. Serve garnished with rosemary.

trout in lemon & red wine sauce

ingredients

SERVES 4

4 trout, cleaned, heads
   removed

225 ml/8 fl oz red wine
   vinegar

300 ml/10 fl oz red wine

150 ml/5 fl oz water

2 bay leaves

4 sprigs fresh thyme

4 sprigs fresh flat-leaf parsley,
   plus extra to garnish

thinly pared rind of 1 lemon

3 shallots, thinly sliced

1 carrot, thinly sliced

12 black peppercorns

8 cloves

salt and pepper

85 g/3 oz unsalted butter,
   diced

1 tbsp chopped fresh flat-leaf
   parsley

1 tbsp snipped fresh dill

method

1 Rinse the fish inside and out under cold running water and pat dry on kitchen paper. Place them in a single layer in a non-metallic dish. Pour the vinegar into a small saucepan and bring to the boil, then pour it over the fish. Set aside to marinate for 30 minutes.

2 Pour the wine and water into a saucepan, add the bay leaves, thyme and parsley sprigs, lemon rind, shallots, carrots, peppercorns and cloves, and season with salt. Bring to the boil over a low heat.

3 Meanwhile, drain the trout and discard the vinegar. Place the fish in a single layer in a large frying pan and strain the wine mixture over them. Cover and simmer over a low heat for 15 minutes, until cooked through and tender. There is no need to turn them.

4 Using a spatula, transfer the trout to individual serving plates and keep warm. Bring the cooking liquid back to the boil and cook until reduced by about three quarters. Gradually beat in the butter, a little at a time, until fully incorporated. Stir in the chopped parsley and dill, taste and adjust the seasoning if necessary. Pour the sauce over the fish, garnish with parsley sprigs and serve immediately.

grilled sardines with lemon sauce

ingredients

SERVES 4

1 large lemon
85 g/3 oz unsalted butter
salt and pepper
20 fresh sardines, cleaned
    and heads removed
1 tbsp chopped fresh fennel
    leaves

method

1 Peel the lemon. Remove all the bitter pith and discard. Using a small, serrated knife, cut between the membranes and ease out the flesh segments, discarding any seeds. Chop finely and set aside.

2 Melt 25 g/1 oz of the butter in a small saucepan and season with salt and pepper. Brush the sardines all over with the melted butter and cook under a preheated grill or on a barbecue, turning once, for 5–6 minutes, until cooked through.

3 Meanwhile, melt the remaining butter, then remove the pan from the heat. Stir in the chopped lemon and fennel.

4 Transfer the sardines to a warmed platter, pour the sauce over them and serve immediately.

linguine with anchovies, olives & capers

ingredients

SERVES 4

sauce

3 tbsp olive oil

2 garlic cloves, finely
    chopped

10 anchovy fillets, drained
    and chopped

140 g/5 oz black olives,
    stoned and chopped

1 tbsp capers, rinsed

450 g/1 lb plum tomatoes,
    peeled, deseeded and
    chopped

pinch of cayenne pepper

salt

400 g/14 oz dried linguine

2 tbsp chopped fresh flat-leaf
    parsley, to garnish

method

1 Heat the olive oil in a heavy-based saucepan. Add the garlic and cook over a low heat, stirring frequently, for 2 minutes. Add the anchovies and mash them to a pulp with a fork. Add the olives, capers and tomatoes and season to taste with cayenne pepper. Cover and simmer for 25 minutes.

2 Meanwhile, bring a pan of lightly salted water to the boil. Add the pasta, bring back to the boil and cook for 8–10 minutes, until tender but still firm to the bite. Drain and transfer to a warmed serving dish.

3 Spoon the anchovy sauce into the dish and toss the pasta, using 2 large forks. Garnish with the parsley and serve immediately.

fillets of sole in tomato & olive sauce

ingredients

SERVES 4

4 tbsp olive oil

900 g/2 lb plum tomatoes, peeled, deseeded and chopped

2 tbsp sun-dried tomato purée

3 garlic cloves, finely chopped

1 tbsp chopped fresh oregano

salt and pepper

85 g/3 oz plain flour

4 sole, filleted

85 g/3 oz unsalted butter

115 g/4 oz black olives, stoned

method

1 Heat the olive oil in a large heavy-based saucepan. Add the tomatoes, tomato purée, garlic and oregano and season to taste with salt and pepper. Stir well, then cover and simmer, stirring occasionally, for 30 minutes, until the mixture is thickened and pulpy.

2 Meanwhile, spread out the flour on a plate and season with salt and pepper. Coat the fish fillets in the seasoned flour, shaking off any excess.

3 Melt half the butter in a heavy-based frying pan. Add as many fillets as the pan will hold in a single layer and cook over a medium heat for 2 minutes on each side. Using a spatula, transfer the fillets to an ovenproof dish and keep warm. Cook the remaining fillets, adding the remaining butter as required.

4 Stir the olives into the tomato sauce, then pour it over the fish. Bake in a preheated oven, 180°C/350°F/Gas Mark 4, for 20 minutes. Serve immediately, straight from the dish.

risotto with sole & tomatoes

ingredients

SERVES 4

3 tbsp butter

3 tbsp olive oil

1 small onion, finely chopped

280 g/10 oz risotto rice

1.2 litres/2 pints simmering
fish or chicken stock

salt and pepper

450 g/1 lb tomatoes, peeled,
deseeded and cut into
strips

6 sun-dried tomatoes
in olive oil, drained and
thinly sliced

3 tbsp tomato purée

50 ml/2 fl oz red wine

450 g/1 lb sole or flounder
fillets, skinned and cut
into strips

115 g/4 oz freshly grated
Parmesan or Grana
Padano cheese

2 tbsp finely chopped fresh
coriander, to garnish

method

1 Melt 2 tablespoons of the butter with
1 tablespoon of the oil in a deep saucepan
over a medium heat. Stir in the onion and
cook, stirring occasionally, for 5 minutes, or
until soft.

2 Reduce the heat, stir in the rice and cook,
stirring constantly, for 2–3 minutes, or until
the grains are translucent. Gradually add
the hot stock, a ladleful at a time, stirring
constantly, until all the liquid is absorbed and
the rice is creamy. Season to taste.

3 Heat the remaining oil in a large heavy-
based frying pan. Add the fresh and sun-dried
tomatoes. Stir well and cook over a medium
heat for 10–15 minutes, or until soft and slushy.
Stir in the tomato purée and wine. Bring the
sauce to the boil, then reduce the heat until it
is just simmering.

4 Add the fish strips to the sauce, stir gently
and cook for 5 minutes, or until the fish flakes
easily. Remove the fish and, if necessary,
increase the heat to reduce the sauce.

5 Remove the risotto from the heat when all
the liquid has been absorbed and stir in the
remaining butter, then the Parmesan. Serve
the risotto with the fish and sauce on top,
garnished with fresh coriander.

sicilian tuna

ingredients

SERVES 4

4 x 140-g/5-oz tuna steaks

2 fennel bulbs, thickly sliced
   lengthways

2 red onions, sliced

2 tbsp virgin olive oil

crusty rolls, to serve

marinade

125 ml/4 fl oz extra virgin
   olive oil

4 garlic cloves, finely
   chopped

4 fresh red chillies, deseeded
   and finely chopped

juice and finely grated rind of
   2 lemons

4 tbsp finely chopped fresh
   flat-leaf parsley

salt and pepper

method

1 First, make the marinade by whisking all the ingredients together in a bowl. Place the tuna steaks in a large shallow dish and spoon over 4 tablespoons of the marinade, turning to coat. Cover and set aside for 30 minutes. Set aside the remaining marinade.

2 Heat a ridged griddle pan. Put the fennel and onions in a bowl, add the oil and toss well to coat. Add to the griddle pan and cook for 5 minutes on each side, until just starting to colour. Transfer to 4 warmed serving plates, drizzle with the reserved marinade and keep warm.

3 Add the tuna steaks to the griddle pan and cook, turning once, for 4–5 minutes, until firm to the touch but still moist inside. Transfer the tuna to the plates and serve immediately with crusty bread.

beans with tuna

ingredients

SERVES 4

800 g/1 lb 12 oz cannellini
  beans, covered and
  soaked overnight in cold
  water
6 tbsp extra virgin olive oil
2 x 200-g/7-oz tuna steaks
2 garlic cloves, lightly crushed
sprig of fresh sage
2 tbsp water
salt and pepper
4 chopped fresh sage leaves,
  to garnish

method

1 Drain the soaked beans and place them in a saucepan. Add enough water to cover and bring to the boil. Reduce the heat and simmer for 1–1¹/2 hours, until tender. Drain the beans thoroughly.

2 Heat 1 tablespoon of the olive oil in a heavy-based frying pan. Add the tuna steaks and cook over a medium heat for 3–4 minutes on each side, until tender. Remove from the pan and set aside to cool.

3 Heat 3 tablespoons of the remaining olive oil in a heavy-based frying pan. Add the garlic and sage sprig and cook briefly over a low heat until the sage starts to sizzle. Remove the garlic and discard.

4 Add the beans and cook for 1 minute, then add the measured water and season to taste with salt and pepper. Cook until the water has been absorbed. Remove and discard the sage sprig, transfer the beans to a bowl and set aside to cool.

5 Meanwhile, flake the tuna, removing any bones. When the beans are lukewarm or at room temperature, according to taste, gently stir in the tuna. Drizzle with the remaining olive oil, sprinkle with the chopped sage and serve.

seafood omelette

ingredients

SERVES 3

2 tbsp unsalted butter

1 tbsp olive oil

1 onion, very finely chopped

175 g/6 oz courgette, halved
    lengthways and sliced

1 celery stick, very finely
    chopped

85 g/3 oz white mushrooms,
    sliced

55 g/2 oz French beans, cut
    into 5-cm/2-inch lengths

4 eggs

85 g/3 oz mascarpone cheese

1 tbsp chopped fresh thyme

1 tbsp shredded fresh basil

salt and pepper

200 g/7 oz canned tuna,
    drained and flaked

115 g/4 oz shelled cooked
    prawns

method

1 Melt the butter with the olive oil in a heavy-based frying pan with a flameproof handle. If the pan has a wooden handle, protect it with foil because it needs to go under the grill. Add the onion and cook over a low heat, stirring occasionally, for 5 minutes, until softened.

2 Add the courgette, celery, mushrooms and beans and cook, stirring occasionally, for a further 8–10 minutes, until starting to brown.

3 Beat the eggs with the mascarpone, thyme, basil, and salt and pepper to taste.

4 Add the tuna to the pan and stir it into the mixture with a wooden spoon, then add the prawns.

5 Pour the egg mixture into the pan and cook for 5 minutes, until it is just starting to set. Draw the egg from the sides of the pan towards the centre to let the uncooked egg run underneath.

6 Put the pan under a preheated grill and cook until the egg is just set and the surface is starting to brown. Cut the omelette into wedges and serve.

tuna with garlic, lemon, capers & olives

ingredients

SERVES 4

350 g/12 oz dried conchiglie
  or gnocchi

4 tbsp olive oil

4 tbsp butter

3 large garlic cloves, thinly
  sliced

200 g/7 oz canned tuna,
  drained and broken into
  chunks

2 tbsp lemon juice

1 tbsp capers, drained

10–12 black olives, stoned
  and sliced

2 tbsp chopped fresh
  flat-leaf parsley, to serve

method

1 Cook the pasta in plenty of boiling salted water until al dente. Drain and return to the saucepan.

2 Heat the olive oil and half the butter in a frying pan over a medium–low heat. Add the garlic and cook for a few seconds, or until just beginning to colour. Reduce the heat to low. Add the tuna, lemon juice, capers and olives. Stir gently until all the ingredients are heated through.

3 Transfer the pasta to a warm serving dish. Pour the tuna mixture over the pasta. Add the parsley and remaining butter. Toss well to mix and serve immediately.

risotto with tuna & pine kernels

ingredients

SERVES 4

3 tbsp butter

4 tbsp olive oil

1 small onion, finely chopped

280 g/10 oz risotto rice

225 g/8 oz tuna, canned and drained, or grilled fresh steaks

1.2 litres/2 pints simmering fish or chicken stock

8–10 black olives, stoned and sliced

1 small pimiento, thinly sliced

1 tsp finely chopped fresh parsley

1 tsp finely chopped fresh marjoram

2 tbsp white wine vinegar

salt and pepper

55 g/2 oz pine kernels

1 garlic clove, chopped

225 g/8 oz fresh tomatoes, peeled, deseeded and diced

85 g/3 oz Parmesan or Grana Padano cheese

method

1 Melt 2 tablespoons of the butter with 1 tablespoon of the oil in a deep saucepan over a medium heat. Add the onion and cook, stirring occasionally, until soft and starting to turn golden. Reduce the heat, add the rice and mix to coat in oil and butter. Cook, stirring constantly, until the grains are translucent. Add the hot stock, a ladleful at a time, stirring constantly, until all the liquid is absorbed and the rice is creamy. Season to taste.

2 While the risotto is cooking, flake the tuna into a bowl and mix in the olives, pimiento, parsley, marjoram and vinegar. Season with salt and pepper.

3 Heat the remaining oil in a small frying pan over a high heat. Add the pine kernels and garlic. Cook, stirring constantly, for 2 minutes, or until they just start to brown. Add the tomatoes and mix well. Continue cooking over a medium heat for 3–4 minutes or until they are thoroughly warm. Pour the tomato mixture over the tuna mixture and mix. Fold into the risotto 5 minutes before the end of the cooking time.

4 Remove the risotto from the heat when all the liquid has been absorbed and add the remaining butter. Mix well, then stir in the Parmesan until it melts. Serve immediately.

bavettine with smoked salmon & rocket

ingredients

SERVES 4

350 g/12 oz dried bavettine

2 tbsp olive oil

1 garlic clove, finely chopped

115 g/4 oz smoked salmon,
    cut into thin strips

55 g/2 oz rocket

salt and pepper

1/2 lemon, to garnish

method

1 Bring a large heavy-based saucepan of lightly salted water to the boil. Add the pasta, return to the boil and cook for 8–10 minutes, or until tender but still firm to the bite.

2 Just before the end of the cooking time, heat the olive oil in a heavy-based frying pan. Add the garlic and cook over a low heat, stirring constantly, for 1 minute. Do not allow the garlic to brown or it will taste bitter. Add the salmon and rocket. Season to taste with salt and pepper and cook, stirring constantly, for 1 minute. Remove the pan from the heat.

3 Drain the pasta and transfer to a warmed serving dish. Add the smoked salmon and rocket mixture, toss lightly and serve, garnished with a lemon half.

layered spaghetti with smoked salmon & prawns

ingredients

SERVES 6

70 g/2¹/₂ oz butter, plus extra
for greasing

350 g/12 oz dried spaghetti

200 g/7 oz smoked salmon,
cut into strips

280 g/10 oz large jumbo
prawns, cooked, peeled
and deveined

1 quantity Béchamel Sauce
(see page 174)

115 g/4 oz freshly grated
Parmesan cheese

method

1 Butter a large ovenproof dish and set aside.

2 Bring a large saucepan of lightly salted water to the boil. Add the pasta, bring back to the boil and cook for 8–10 minutes, until tender but still firm to the bite. Drain well, return to the pan, add 55 g/2 oz of the butter and toss well.

3 Spoon half the spaghetti into the prepared dish, cover with the strips of smoked salmon, then top with the prawns. Pour over half the béchamel sauce and sprinkle with half the Parmesan. Add the remaining spaghetti, cover with the remaining sauce and sprinkle with the remaining Parmesan. Dice the remaining butter and dot it over the surface.

4 Bake in a preheated oven, 180°C/350°F/Gas Mark 4, for 15 minutes, until the top is golden. Serve immediately.

springtime pasta

ingredients

SERVES 4

2 tbsp lemon juice

4 baby globe artichokes

7 tbsp olive oil

2 shallots, finely chopped

2 garlic cloves, finely
    chopped

2 tbsp chopped fresh flat-leaf
    parsley

2 tbsp chopped fresh mint

350 g/12 oz dried rigatoni or
    other tubular pasta

12 large raw prawns

25 g/1 oz unsalted butter

salt and pepper

method

1 Fill a bowl with cold water and add the lemon juice. Prepare the artichokes one at a time. Cut off the stems and trim away any tough outer leaves. Cut across the tops of the leaves. Slice in half lengthways and remove the central fibrous chokes, then cut lengthways into 5-mm/1/4-inch thick slices. Place the slices in the bowl of acidulated water to prevent discoloration.

2 Heat 5 tablespoons of the olive oil in a heavy-based frying pan. Drain the artichoke slices and pat dry with kitchen paper. Add them to the pan with the shallots, garlic, parsley and mint, and cook over a low heat, stirring frequently, for 10–12 minutes until tender.

3 Meanwhile, bring a large saucepan of lightly salted water to the boil. Add the pasta, bring back to the boil and cook for 8–10 minutes, until tender but still firm to the bite.

4 Peel the prawns, cut a slit along the back of each and remove and discard the dark vein. Melt the butter in a small frying pan, cut the prawns in half and add them to the pan. Cook, stirring occasionally, for 2–3 minutes, until they have changed colour. Season to taste.

5 Drain the pasta and pour it into a bowl. Add the remaining olive oil and toss well. Add the artichoke mixture and the prawns and toss again. Serve immediately.

macaroni & seafood bake

ingredients

SERVES 4

350 g/12 oz dried
    short-cut macaroni

6 tbsp butter, plus extra for
    greasing

2 small fennel bulbs,
    thinly sliced

175 g/6 oz mushrooms, thinly
    sliced

175 g/6 oz cooked
    peeled prawns

pinch of cayenne pepper

300 ml/10 fl oz Béchamel
    Sauce (see page 174)

55 g/2 oz freshly grated
    Parmesan cheese

2 large tomatoes, sliced

olive oil, for brushing

1 tsp dried oregano

method

1 Bring a large saucepan of lightly salted water to the boil. Add the pasta, return to the boil and cook for 8–10 minutes, or until tender but still firm to the bite. Drain and return to the pan. Add 2 tablespoons of the butter to the pasta, cover, shake the pan and keep warm.

2 Melt the remaining butter in a separate saucepan. Add the fennel and cook for 3–4 minutes. Stir in the mushrooms and cook for a further 2 minutes. Stir in the prawns, then remove the pan from the heat. Stir the cayenne pepper into the béchamel sauce and add the prawn mixture and pasta.

3 Grease a large ovenproof dish with butter, then pour the mixture into the dish and spread evenly. Sprinkle over the Parmesan cheese and arrange the tomato slices in a ring around the edge. Brush the tomatoes with olive oil, then sprinkle over the oregano. Bake in a preheated oven, 180°C/350°F/Gas Mark 4 for 25 minutes, or until golden brown. Serve immediately.

prawn & asparagus risotto

ingredients

SERVES 4

1.2 litres/2 pints vegetable
   stock
375 g/12 oz fresh asparagus
   spears, cut into 5-cm/
   2-inch lengths
2 tbsp olive oil
1 onion, finely chopped
1 garlic clove, finely chopped
350 g/12 oz risotto rice
450 g/1 lb raw jumbo prawns,
   peeled and deveined
2 tbsp olive paste or tapenade
2 tbsp chopped fresh basil
salt and pepper
fresh Parmesan cheese
fresh basil sprigs, to garnish

method

1 Bring the stock to the boil in a large saucepan. Add the asparagus and cook for 3 minutes until just tender. Strain, reserving the stock, and refresh the asparagus under cold running water. Drain and set aside.

2 Return the stock to the pan and keep simmering gently over a low heat while you are cooking the risotto.

3 Heat the olive oil in a large heavy-based saucepan. Add the onion and cook over a medium heat, stirring occasionally, for 5 minutes until softened. Add the garlic and cook for a further 30 seconds.

4 Reduce the heat, add the rice and mix to coat in oil. Cook, stirring constantly, for 2–3 minutes, or until the grains are translucent.

5 Gradually add the hot stock, a ladleful at a time. Stir constantly and add more liquid as the rice absorbs each addition. Increase the heat to medium so that the liquid bubbles. Cook for 20 minutes, until all the liquid is absorbed and the rice is creamy. Add the prawns and asparagus with the last ladleful of stock.

6 Remove the pan from the heat, stir in the olive paste and basil and season to taste with salt and pepper. Serve the risotto immediately, sprinkled with Parmesan cheese and garnished with basil sprigs.

scallops with porcini & cream sauce

ingredients

SERVES 4

25 g/1 oz dried porcini
    mushrooms

500 ml/18 fl oz hot water

3 tbsp olive oil

3 tbsp butter

350 g/12 oz scallops, sliced

2 garlic cloves, very finely
    chopped

2 tbsp lemon juice

250 ml/9 fl oz double cream

salt and pepper

350 g/12 oz dried fettuccine
    or pappardelle

2 tbsp chopped fresh
    flat-leaf parsley

method

1 Put the porcini and hot water in a bowl and soak for 20 minutes. Strain the mushrooms, reserving the soaking water, and chop roughly. Line a sieve with kitchen paper and strain the mushroom water into a bowl.

2 Heat the oil and butter in a large frying pan over a medium heat. Add the scallops and cook for 2 minutes, or until just golden. Add the garlic and mushrooms, then stir-fry for another minute.

3 Stir in the lemon juice, cream and 150 ml/ 5 fl oz of the mushroom water. Bring to the boil, then simmer over a medium heat for 2–3 minutes, stirring constantly, until the liquid is reduced by half. Season with salt and pepper. Remove from the heat.

4 Cook the pasta in plenty of boiling salted water until al dente. Drain and transfer to a warm serving dish. Briefly reheat the sauce and pour over the pasta. Sprinkle with the parsley and toss well to mix. Serve immediately.

saffron & lemon risotto with scallops

ingredients

SERVES 4

16 live scallops, shucked

juice of 1 lemon, plus extra
for seasoning

3 tbsp butter

1 tbsp olive oil, plus extra
for brushing

1 small onion, finely chopped

280 g/10 oz risotto rice

1 tsp crumbled saffron
threads

1.2 litres/2 pints simmering
fish or vegetable stock

salt and pepper

2 tbsp vegetable oil

115 g/4 oz freshly grated
Parmesan or Grana
Padano cheese

1 lemon, cut into wedges

2 tsp grated lemon zest,
to garnish

method

1 Place the scallops in a non-metallic bowl and mix with the lemon juice. Cover the bowl with clingfilm and chill for 15 minutes.

2 Melt 2 tablespoons of the butter with the oil in a deep saucepan over a medium heat. Add the onion and cook, stirring occasionally, until soft and starting to turn golden. Add the rice and mix to coat in oil and butter. Cook, stirring, until the grains are translucent. Dissolve the saffron in 4 tablespoons of hot stock and add to the rice. Gradually add the remaining stock a ladleful at a time, stirring constantly, until all the liquid is absorbed and the rice is creamy. Season with salt and pepper.

3 When the risotto is nearly cooked, heat a griddle pan over a high heat. Brush the scallops with oil and sear on the griddle pan for 3–4 minutes on each side, depending on their thickness. Take care not to overcook or they will be rubbery.

4 Remove the risotto from the heat and add the remaining butter. Mix well, then stir in the Parmesan until it melts. Season with lemon juice, adding just 1 teaspoon at a time and tasting as you go. Serve the risotto immediately with the scallops and lemon wedges arranged on top, sprinkled with lemon zest.

risotto with squid & garlic butter

ingredients

SERVES 4

8–12 raw baby squid,
    cleaned, rinsed and dried
150 g/5^1/$_2$ oz butter
1 tbsp olive oil
1 small onion, finely chopped
280 g/10 oz risotto rice
1.2 litres/2 pints simmering
    fish or chicken stock
salt and pepper
3 garlic cloves, crushed
85 g/3 oz freshly grated
    Parmesan or Grana
    Padano cheese
2 tbsp finely chopped fresh
    parsley, to garnish

method

1 Cut the squid in half lengthways, then score with a sharp knife, making horizontal and vertical cuts. Dice the larger tentacles.

2 Melt 2 tablespoons of the butter with the oil in a deep saucepan over a medium heat. Cook the onion, stirring, until soft and starting to turn golden. Stir in the rice and cook, stirring, until the grains are translucent. Gradually add the hot stock, a ladleful at a time. Stir constantly and add more liquid as the rice absorbs each addition. Cook for 20 minutes, or until all the liquid is absorbed and the rice is creamy. Season with salt and pepper.

3 When the risotto is nearly cooked, melt 115 g/ 4 oz of the remaining butter in a heavy-based frying pan. Add the garlic and cook over a low heat until soft. Increase the heat to high, add the squid and toss to cook for no more than 2–3 minutes or the squid will become tough. Remove the squid from the pan, draining carefully and reserving the garlic butter.

4 Remove the risotto from the heat and stir in the remaining butter, then the Parmesan. Spoon onto warmed serving plates and arrange the squid on top. Spoon some of the garlic butter over each portion. Serve immediately, sprinkled with the parsley.

shellfish bake

ingredients

SERVES 6

350 g/12 oz dried conchiglie

6 tbsp butter, plus extra
    for greasing

2 fennel bulbs, thinly sliced

175 g/6 oz mushrooms, thinly
    sliced

175 g/6 oz cooked,
    peeled prawns

175 g/6 oz cooked crabmeat

pinch of cayenne pepper

300 ml/10 fl oz Béchamel
    Sauce (see page 174)

55 g/2 oz freshly grated
    Parmesan cheese

2 beefsteak tomatoes, sliced

olive oil, for brushing

green salad and crusty bread,
    to serve

method

1 Bring a large heavy-based saucepan of lightly salted water to the boil. Add the pasta, return to the boil and cook for 8–10 minutes, or until tender but still firm to the bite. Drain the pasta well, return to the pan and stir in 2 tablespoons of the butter. Cover the pan and keep warm.

2 Meanwhile, melt the remaining butter in a large heavy-based frying pan. Add the fennel and cook over a medium heat for 5 minutes, or until softened. Stir in the mushrooms and cook for a further 2 minutes. Stir in the prawns and crabmeat, cook for a further 1 minute, then remove the pan from the heat.

3 Grease 6 small ovenproof dishes with butter. Stir the cayenne pepper into the béchamel sauce, add the shellfish mixture and pasta, then spoon into the prepared dishes. Sprinkle with the Parmesan cheese and arrange the tomato slices on top, then brush the tomatoes with a little olive oil.

4 Bake in a preheated oven, 180°C/350°F/Gas Mark 4, for 25 minutes, or until golden brown. Serve hot with a green salad and crusty bread.

spaghetti with clams

ingredients

SERVES 4

1 kg/2 lb 4 oz live clams

175 ml/6 fl oz water

175 ml/6 fl oz dry white wine

350 g/12 oz dried spaghetti

5 tbsp olive oil

2 garlic cloves, finely
    chopped

4 tbsp chopped fresh flat-leaf
    parsley

salt and pepper

method

1 Place the clams in a large heavy-based saucepan, add the water and wine, cover and cook over a high heat, shaking the saucepan occasionally, for 5 minutes, or until the shells have opened.

2 Remove the clams with a slotted spoon and cool slightly. Strain the cooking liquid into a small saucepan through a sieve lined with muslin. Bring to the boil and cook until reduced by about half, then remove from the heat. Meanwhile, discard any clams that have not opened, then remove the remainder from their shells and reserve until required.

3 Bring a large saucepan of lightly salted water to the boil. Add the pasta, return to the boil and cook for 8–10 minutes, or until tender but still firm to the bite.

4 Meanwhile, heat the olive oil in a large heavy-based frying pan. Add the garlic and cook, stirring frequently, for 2 minutes. Add the parsley and the reduced clam cooking liquid and simmer gently.

5 Drain the pasta and add it to the frying pan with the clams. Season with salt and pepper and cook, stirring constantly, for 4 minutes, or until the pasta is coated and the clams have heated through. Transfer to a warmed serving dish and serve immediately.

seafood pizza

ingredients

SERVES 2

1 quantity Pizza Dough (see page 200)

plain flour, for dusting

virgin olive oil, for oiling and drizzling

1 quantity Tomato Sauce (see page 80)

225 g/8 oz mixed fresh seafood, including cooked prawns, cooked mussels and squid rings

1/2 red pepper, deseeded and chopped

1/2 yellow pepper, deseeded and chopped

1 tbsp capers, rinsed

55 g/2 oz Taleggio cheese, grated

3 tbsp freshly grated Parmesan cheese

1/2 tsp dried oregano

75 g/2³/4 oz anchovy fillets in oil, drained and sliced

10 black olives, stoned

salt and pepper

method

1 Turn out the prepared pizza dough onto a lightly floured work surface and knock down. Knead briefly, then roll out the dough into a circle about 5 mm/1/4 inch thick. Transfer to a lightly oiled baking sheet and push up the edge with your fingers to form a small rim.

2 Spread the tomato sauce over the pizza base, almost to the edge. Arrange the mixed seafood, red and yellow peppers and capers evenly on top.

3 Sprinkle the Taleggio, Parmesan and oregano evenly over the topping. Add the anchovy fillets and olives, drizzle with olive oil and season to taste with salt and pepper.

4 Bake in a preheated oven, 220°C/425°F/ Gas Mark 7, for 20–25 minutes, until the crust is crisp and the cheese has melted. Serve immediately.

vegetable dishes

Italian cuisine is ideal for those who like their food to centre around vegetables cooked in interesting and innovative ways. It is a well-known fact that the Mediterranean diet is an exceptionally nutritious one, and this is largely because of the wide selection of intensely coloured vegetables, including aubergines, tomatoes, courgettes, artichokes and peppers, which combine with extra virgin olive oil to promote a healthy heart and tales of remarkable longevity.

This chapter has some warming and filling winter dishes, baked in the oven, as well as some light and delicious risotto recipes made vibrant in taste and colour by glorious summer vegetables. A really good Parmesan cheese is the perfect ingredient to finish off a vegetable risotto (and indeed many Italian dishes) – by law, this most famous of Italian cheeses can be produced only in a tightly defined zone around Parma. Look for the words 'Parmigiano Reggiano' and you will know that you have the real thing. Keep the cheese wrapped in aluminium foil in the refrigerator and grate it freshly as required.

You will also find some mouthwatering pasta recipes in this chapter – pasta, again, lends itself to some excellent vegetable-based dishes, many of which are very quick and easy to prepare.

aubergines with mozzarella & parmesan

ingredients

SERVES 6–8

3 aubergines, thinly sliced

olive oil, for brushing

300 g/10½ oz buffalo
    mozzarella, sliced

115 g/4 oz freshly grated
    Parmesan cheese

3 tbsp dried, uncoloured
    breadcrumbs

1 tbsp butter

sprigs fresh flat-leaf parsley,
    to garnish

tomato and basil sauce

2 tbsp virgin olive oil

4 shallots, finely chopped

2 garlic cloves, finely
    chopped

400 g/14 oz canned tomatoes

1 tsp sugar

salt and pepper

8 fresh basil leaves, shredded

method

1 Arrange the aubergine slices in a single layer on one or two large baking sheets. Brush with olive oil and bake in a preheated oven, 200°C/400°F/Gas Mark 6, for 15–20 minutes, until tender but not collapsing.

2 Meanwhile, make the tomato and basil sauce. Heat the oil in a heavy-based saucepan, add the shallots and cook, stirring occasionally, for 5 minutes, until softened. Add the garlic and cook for 1 minute more. Add the tomatoes, with their can juices, and break them up with a wooden spoon. Stir in the sugar and season to taste with salt and pepper. Bring to the boil, reduce the heat and simmer for about 10 minutes, until thickened. Stir in the basil leaves.

3 Brush an ovenproof dish with olive oil and arrange half the aubergine slices in the bottom. Cover with half the mozzarella, spoon over half the tomato sauce and sprinkle with half the Parmesan. Mix the remaining Parmesan with the breadcrumbs. Repeat the layers, ending with the Parmesan mixture.

4 Dot the top with butter and bake for 25 minutes, until the topping is golden brown. Remove from the oven and let stand for 5 minutes before slicing and serving, garnished with the parsley.

aubergine & tomato bake

ingredients

SERVES 4

600 g/1 lb 5 oz aubergine,
  cut into 1-cm/$\frac{1}{2}$ -inch
  thick slices

salt and pepper

225 ml/8 fl oz olive oil

600 g/1 lb 5 oz plum
  tomatoes, cut into 1-cm/
  $\frac{1}{2}$ -inch thick slices

55 g/2 oz freshly grated
  Parmesan cheese

2 tbsp fresh white
  breadcrumbs

method

1 To remove any bitterness, layer the aubergine slices in a colander, sprinkling each layer with salt. Stand the colander in the sink and drain for 30 minutes. Meanwhile, spread out the tomato slices on kitchen paper, cover with more kitchen paper and drain. Rinse the aubergine thoroughly under cold running water to remove all traces of the salt, then pat dry with kitchen paper.

2 Heat 2 tablespoons of the olive oil in a large heavy-based frying pan. Add the tomato slices and cook for just 30 seconds on each side. Transfer to a large platter and season to taste.

3 Wipe out the frying pan with kitchen paper, then add 2 tablespoons of the remaining olive oil and heat. Add the aubergine slices, in batches, and cook on both sides until golden brown. Remove from the pan and drain on kitchen paper. Cook the remaining slices in the same way, adding more olive oil as required.

4 Brush a large ovenproof dish with some of the remaining olive oil. Arrange alternate layers of aubergine and tomatoes, sprinkling each layer with Parmesan cheese. Top with the breadcrumbs and drizzle with the remaining olive oil. Bake in a preheated oven, 180°C/350°F/Gas Mark 4, for 25–30 minutes, until golden. Serve immediately.

spinach & ricotta dumplings

ingredients

SERVES 4

1 kg/2 lb 4 oz fresh spinach,
coarse stalks removed

350 g/12 oz ricotta cheese

115 g/4 oz freshly grated
Parmesan cheese

3 eggs, lightly beaten

pinch of freshly grated
nutmeg

salt and pepper

115–175 g/4–6 oz plain flour,
plus extra for dusting

herb butter

115 g/4 oz unsalted butter

2 tbsp chopped fresh oregano

2 tbsp chopped fresh sage

method

1 Wash the spinach, place it in a saucepan with just the water clinging to its leaves, cover and cook over a low heat for 6–8 minutes, until just wilted. Drain well and set aside to cool.

2 Squeeze out as much liquid as possible from the spinach, then chop finely. Place the spinach in a bowl, add the ricotta, half the Parmesan, the eggs and nutmeg, season to taste and beat until thoroughly combined. Sift in 115 g/4 oz of the flour and lightly work it into the mixture, adding more if necessary, to make a workable mixture. Cover with clingfilm and chill for 1 hour.

3 With floured hands, break off small pieces of the mixture and roll them carefully into walnut-sized balls – they are quite delicate. Lightly dust the dumplings with flour.

4 Bring a large saucepan of lightly salted water to the boil. Add the dumplings and cook for 2–3 minutes, until they rise to the surface. Remove them from the pan with a slotted spoon, drain well and set aside.

5 To make the herb butter, melt the butter in a large heavy-based frying pan. Add the oregano and sage and cook over a low heat, stirring frequently, for 1 minute. Add the dumplings and toss gently for 1 minute to coat. Serve sprinkled with the remaining Parmesan.

spinach & ricotta ravioli

ingredients

SERVES 4

350 g/12 oz fresh spinach
    leaves, coarse stalks
    removed

225 g/8 oz ricotta cheese

55 g/2 oz freshly grated
    Parmesan cheese

2 eggs, lightly beaten

pinch of freshly grated
    nutmeg

pepper

plain flour, for dusting

freshly grated Parmesan
    cheese, to serve

spinach
pasta dough

175 g/6 oz plain flour, plus
    extra for dusting

pinch of salt

225 g/8 oz frozen spinach,
    thawed, squeezed dry
    and finely chopped

2 eggs, lightly beaten

1 tbsp olive oil

method

1 To make the pasta dough, sift the flour into a food processor and add the salt. Add the chopped spinach, then pour in the eggs and olive oil and process until the dough begins to come together. Turn out onto a lightly floured work surface and knead until smooth. Wrap in clingfilm and set aside for at least 30 minutes.

2 Cook the spinach, with just the water clinging to the leaves after washing, over a low heat for 5 minutes until wilted. Drain and squeeze out as much moisture as possible. Cool, then chop finely. Beat the ricotta cheese until smooth, then stir in the spinach, Parmesan and half the egg and season to taste with nutmeg and pepper.

3 Halve the pasta dough. Cover one piece and thinly roll out the other on a floured work surface. Cover and roll out the second piece. Put small mounds of filling in rows 4 cm/ 1 1/2 inches apart on one sheet of dough and brush the spaces in between with the remaining beaten egg. Fit the second piece of dough on top. Press down between the mounds, pushing out any air. Cut into squares and rest on a tea towel for 1 hour.

4 Bring a large saucepan of salted water to the boil, add the ravioli, in batches, return to the boil, and cook for 5 minutes. Remove with a slotted spoon and drain on kitchen paper. Serve with grated Parmesan cheese.

radiatori with pumpkin sauce

ingredients

SERVES 4

55 g/2 oz unsalted butter

115 g/4 oz onions
    or shallots, very finely
    chopped

salt

800 g/1 lb 12 oz pumpkin,
    unprepared weight

pinch of freshly grated
    nutmeg

350 g/12 oz dried radiatori

200 ml/7 fl oz single cream

4 tbsp freshly grated
    Parmesan cheese,
    plus extra to serve

2 tbsp chopped fresh flat-leaf
    parsley

salt and pepper

method

1 Melt the butter in a heavy-based saucepan over a low heat. Add the onions, sprinkle with a little salt, cover and cook, stirring frequently, for 25–30 minutes.

2 Scoop out and discard the seeds from the pumpkin. Peel and finely chop the flesh. Add the pumpkin to the pan and season to taste with nutmeg. Cover and cook over a low heat, stirring occasionally, for 45 minutes.

3 Meanwhile, bring a large saucepan of lightly salted water to the boil. Add the pasta, bring back to the boil and cook for 8–10 minutes, until tender but still firm to the bite. Drain thoroughly, reserving about 150 ml/5 fl oz of the cooking liquid.

4 Stir the cream, grated Parmesan and parsley into the pumpkin sauce and season to taste with salt and pepper. If the mixture seems a little too thick, add some or all of the reserved cooking liquid. Pour in the pasta and toss for 1 minute. Serve immediately, with extra Parmesan for sprinkling.

vegetarian lasagne

ingredients

SERVES 4

olive oil, for brushing

2 aubergines, sliced

2 tbsp butter

1 garlic clove, finely chopped

4 courgettes, sliced

1 tbsp finely chopped fresh
flat-leaf parsley

1 tbsp finely chopped fresh
marjoram

225 g/8 oz mozzarella
cheese, grated

400 g/14 oz strained canned
tomatoes

175 g/6 oz dried no-precook
lasagne

salt and pepper

600 ml/1 pint Béchamel
Sauce (see page 174)

55 g/2 oz freshly grated
Parmesan cheese

method

1 Brush a large ovenproof dish with olive oil. Brush a large griddle pan with olive oil and heat until smoking. Add half the aubergine slices and cook over a medium heat for 8 minutes, or until golden brown all over. Remove the aubergine from the griddle pan and drain on kitchen paper. Add the remaining aubergine slices and extra oil, if necessary, and cook for 8 minutes, or until golden brown all over.

2 Melt the butter in a frying pan and add the garlic, courgettes, parsley and marjoram. Cook over a medium heat, stirring frequently, for 5 minutes, or until the courgettes are golden brown all over. Remove from the pan and let drain on kitchen paper.

3 Layer the aubergine, courgettes, mozzarella, strained tomatoes and lasagne in the dish, seasoning with salt and pepper as you go and finishing with a layer of lasagne. Pour over the béchamel sauce, making sure that all the pasta is covered. Sprinkle with the grated Parmesan cheese and bake in a preheated oven, 200°C/400°F/Gas Mark 6, for 30–40 minutes, or until golden brown. Serve the lasagne immediately.

mixed vegetable agnolotti

ingredients

SERVES 4

butter, for greasing

1 quantity basic pasta dough
(see page 164, omitting
spinach from the recipe)

plain flour, for dusting

85 g/3 oz freshly grated
Parmesan cheese

mixed salad leaves, to serve

filling

125 ml/4 fl oz olive oil

1 red onion, chopped

3 garlic cloves, chopped

2 large aubergines,
cut into chunks

3 large courgettes, cut into
chunks

6 beefsteak tomatoes,
peeled, deseeded and
roughly chopped

1 large green pepper,
deseeded and diced

1 large red pepper, deseeded
and diced

1 tbsp sun-dried tomato
purée

1 tbsp shredded fresh basil

salt and pepper

method

1 To make the filling, heat the olive oil in a large heavy-based saucepan. Add the onion and garlic and cook over a low heat, stirring occasionally, for 5 minutes, or until softened. Add the aubergine, courgettes, tomatoes, green and red peppers, sun-dried tomato purée and basil. Season to taste with salt and pepper, cover and simmer gently, stirring occasionally, for 20 minutes.

2 Lightly grease an ovenproof dish with butter. Roll out the pasta dough on a lightly floured work surface and stamp out 7.5-cm/3-inch circles with a plain cutter. Place a spoonful of the vegetable filling on one side of each circle. Dampen the edges slightly and fold the pasta circles over, pressing together to seal.

3 Bring a large pan of lightly salted water to the boil. Add the agnolotti, in batches if necessary, return to the boil and cook for 3–4 minutes. Remove with a slotted spoon, drain and transfer to the dish. Sprinkle with the Parmesan cheese and bake in a preheated oven, 200°C/400°F/Gas Mark 6, for 20 minutes. Serve with salad leaves.

penne in a creamy mushroom sauce

ingredients

SERVES 4

4 tbsp butter

1 tbsp olive oil

6 shallots, sliced

450 g/1 lb chestnut
    mushrooms, sliced

salt and pepper

1 tsp plain flour

150 ml/5 fl oz double cream
    or panna da cucina

2 tbsp port

115 g/4 oz sun-dried
    tomatoes in oil, drained
    and chopped

pinch of freshly grated
    nutmeg

350 g/12 oz dried penne

2 tbsp chopped fresh
    flat-leaf parsley

method

1 Melt the butter with the olive oil in a large heavy-based frying pan. Add the shallots and cook over a low heat, stirring occasionally, for 4–5 minutes, or until softened. Add the mushrooms and cook over a low heat for a further 2 minutes. Season to taste with salt and pepper, sprinkle in the flour and cook, stirring, for 1 minute.

2 Remove the pan from the heat and gradually stir in the cream and port. Return to the heat, add the sun-dried tomatoes and grated nutmeg and cook over a low heat, stirring occasionally, for 8 minutes.

3 Meanwhile, bring a large heavy-based saucepan of lightly salted water to the boil. Add the pasta, return to the boil and cook for 8–10 minutes, or until tender but still firm to the bite. Drain the pasta well and add to the mushroom sauce. Cook for 3 minutes, then transfer to a warmed serving dish. Sprinkle with the parsley and serve immediately.

baked pasta with mushrooms

ingredients

SERVES 4

140 g/5 oz fontina cheese, thinly sliced

85 g/3 oz butter, plus extra for greasing

350 g/12 oz mixed exotic mushrooms, sliced

350 g/12 oz dried tagliatelle

2 egg yolks

salt and pepper

4 tbsp freshly grated pecorino cheese

béchamel sauce

55 g/2 oz unsalted butter

55 g/2 oz plain flour

500 ml/18 fl oz milk

1 bay leaf

salt and pepper

pinch of freshly grated nutmeg

method

1 To make the béchamel sauce, melt the butter, add the flour and cook over a low heat, stirring constantly, for 1 minute. Gradually stir in the milk then bring to the boil, stirring constantly, until thickened and smooth. Add the bay leaf and simmer gently for 2 minutes. Remove the bay leaf and season the sauce to taste with salt, pepper and nutmeg. Remove the pan from the heat.

2 Stir the fontina cheese into the sauce and set aside.Melt 25 g/1 oz of the butter in a large saucepan. Add the mushrooms and cook over a low heat, stirring occasionally, for 10 minutes.

3 Meanwhile, bring a large saucepan of lightly salted water to the boil. Add the pasta, bring back to the boil and cook for 8–10 minutes, until tender but still firm to the bite. Drain, return to the pan and add the remaining butter, the egg yolks and about one third of the béchamel sauce, then season to taste. Toss well to mix, then gently stir in the mushrooms.

4 Lightly grease a large ovenproof dish and spoon in the pasta mixture. Pour over the remaining sauce evenly and sprinkle with the pecorino. Bake in a preheated oven, 200°C/400°F/Gas Mark 6, for 15–20 minutes, until golden brown. Serve immediately.

mushroom cannelloni

ingredients

SERVES 4

2 dried cannelloni tubes
2 tbsp butter
450 g/1 lb mixed wild
    mushrooms, finely
    chopped
1 garlic clove, finely chopped
85 g/3 oz fresh breadcrumbs
150 ml/5 fl oz milk
4 tbsp olive oil, plus extra
    for brushing
225 g/8 oz ricotta cheese
6 tbsp freshly grated
    Parmesan cheese
salt and pepper
2 tbsp pine kernels
2 tbsp flaked almonds

tomato sauce

2 tbsp olive oil
1 onion, finely chopped
1 garlic clove, finely chopped
800 g/1 lb 12 oz canned
    chopped tomatoes
1 tbsp tomato purée
8 black olives, stoned and
    chopped
salt and pepper

method

1 Bring a large saucepan of lightly salted water to the boil. Add the cannelloni tubes, return to the boil and cook for 8–10 minutes, or until tender but still firm to the bite. With a slotted spoon, transfer the cannelloni tubes to a plate and pat dry.

2 Meanwhile, make the tomato sauce. Heat the olive oil in a frying pan. Add the onion and garlic and cook over a low heat for 5 minutes, or until softened. Add the tomatoes and their can juices, tomato purée and olives and season to taste. Bring to the boil and cook for 3–4 minutes. Pour the sauce into a large ovenproof dish brushed with olive oil.

3 To make the filling, melt the butter in a heavy-based frying pan. Add the mushrooms and garlic and cook over a medium heat, stirring frequently, for 3–5 minutes, or until tender. Remove the pan from the heat. Mix the breadcrumbs, milk and olive oil together in a large bowl, then stir in the ricotta, mushroom mixture and 4 tablespoons of the Parmesan cheese. Season to taste with salt and pepper.

4 Fill the cannelloni tubes with the mushroom mixture and place them in the dish. Brush with olive oil and sprinkle with the remaining Parmesan cheese, pine kernels and almonds. Bake in a preheated oven, 190°C/375°F/Gas Mark 5, for 25 minutes, or until golden.

fusilli with gorgonzola & mushroom sauce

ingredients

SERVES 4

350 g/12 oz dried fusilli

3 tbsp olive oil

350 g/12 oz exotic
    mushrooms, sliced

1 garlic clove, finely chopped

400 ml/14 fl oz double cream

250 g/9 oz Gorgonzola
    cheese, crumbled

salt and pepper

2 tbsp chopped fresh flat-leaf
    parsley, to garnish

method

1 Bring a large saucepan of lightly salted water to the boil. Add the pasta, bring back to the boil and cook for 8–10 minutes, until tender but still firm to the bite.

2 Meanwhile, heat the olive oil in a heavy-based saucepan. Add the mushrooms and cook over a low heat, stirring frequently, for 5 minutes. Add the garlic and cook for a further 2 minutes.

3 Add the cream, bring to the boil and cook for 1 minute, until slightly thickened. Stir in the cheese and cook over a low heat until it has melted. Do not let the sauce boil once the cheese has been added. Season to taste with salt and pepper and remove the pan from the heat.

4 Drain the pasta and pour it into a serving bowl. Pour the sauce over the pasta then serve immediately, garnished with the parsley.

penne with pepper & goat's cheese sauce

ingredients

SERVES 4

2 tbsp olive oil

1 tbsp butter

1 small onion, finely chopped

4 peppers, yellow and red,
deseeded and cut into
2-cm/³/4-inch squares

3 garlic cloves, thinly sliced

salt and pepper

450 g/1 lb dried rigatoni or
penne

125 g/4¹/2 oz goat's cheese,
crumbled

15 fresh basil leaves,
shredded

10 black olives, stoned and
sliced

method

1 Heat the oil and butter in a large frying pan over a medium heat. Add the onion and cook until soft. Raise the heat to medium–high and add the peppers and garlic. Cook for 12–15 minutes, stirring, until the peppers are tender but not mushy. Season with salt and pepper. Remove from the heat.

2 Cook the pasta in plenty of boiling salted water until al dente. Drain and transfer to a warm serving dish. Add the goat's cheese and toss to mix.

3 Briefly reheat the sauce. Add the basil and olives. Pour over the pasta and toss well to mix. Serve immediately.

spaghetti with roasted garlic & pepper sauce

ingredients

SERVES 4

6 large garlic cloves,
    unpeeled

400 g/14 oz bottled roasted
    red peppers, drained and
    sliced

200 g/7 oz canned chopped
    tomatoes

3 tbsp olive oil

1/4 tsp dried chilli flakes

1 tsp chopped fresh thyme or
    oregano

salt and pepper

350 g/12 oz dried spaghetti,
    bucatini or linguine

freshly grated Parmesan,
    to serve

method

1 Place the unpeeled garlic cloves in a shallow, ovenproof dish. Roast in a preheated oven, 200°C/400°F/Gas Mark 6, for 7–10 minutes, or until the cloves feel soft.

2 Put the peppers, tomatoes and oil in a food processor or blender, then purée. Squeeze the garlic flesh into the purée. Add the chilli flakes and oregano. Season with salt and pepper. Blend again, then scrape into a saucepan and set aside.

3 Cook the pasta in plenty of boiling salted water until al dente. Drain and transfer to a warm serving dish.

4 Reheat the sauce and pour over the pasta. Toss well to mix. Serve immediately with Parmesan.

hot chilli pasta

ingredients

SERVES 4

150 ml/5 fl oz dry white wine

1 tbsp sun-dried
tomato purée

2 fresh red chillies

2 garlic cloves,
finely chopped

350 g/12 oz dried tortiglioni

salt and pepper

4 tbsp chopped fresh
flat-leaf parsley

fresh pecorino cheese
shavings, to garnish

sugocasa

5 tbsp extra virgin olive oil

450 g/1 lb plum tomatoes,
chopped

salt and pepper

method

1 First make the sugocasa. Heat the olive oil in a frying pan until it is almost smoking. Add the tomatoes and cook over a high heat for 2–3 minutes. Reduce the heat to low and cook gently for 20 minutes, or until very soft. Season to taste with salt and pepper, then pass through a food mill or blender into a clean saucepan.

2 Add the wine, sun-dried tomato purée, whole chillies and garlic to the sugocasa and bring to the boil. Reduce the heat and simmer gently.

3 Meanwhile, bring a large saucepan of lightly salted water to the boil. Add the pasta, return to the boil and cook for 8–10 minutes, or until tender but still firm to the bite.

4 Meanwhile, remove the chillies and taste the sauce. If you prefer a hotter flavour, chop some or all of the chillies and return them to the pan. Check the seasoning at the same time, then stir in half the parsley.

5 Drain the pasta and tip it into a warmed serving bowl. Add the sauce and toss to coat. Sprinkle with the remaining parsley, garnish with the pecorino shavings and serve immediately.

minted green risotto

ingredients

SERVES 6

2 tbsp butter

225 g/8 oz shelled fresh peas
or thawed frozen peas

250 g/9 oz fresh young
spinach leaves, washed
and drained

1 bunch of fresh mint, leaves
stripped from stalks

2 tbsp chopped fresh basil

2 tbsp chopped fresh oregano

pinch of freshly grated
nutmeg

4 tbsp mascarpone cheese

2 tbsp vegetable oil

1 onion, finely chopped

2 celery sticks, including
leaves, finely chopped

2 garlic cloves, finely
chopped

$1/2$ tsp dried thyme

300 g/$10^{1}/_{2}$ oz risotto rice

50 ml/2 fl oz dry white
vermouth

1 litre/$1^{3}/_{4}$ pints simmering
chicken or vegetable stock

85 g/3 oz freshly grated
Parmesan cheese

method

1 Heat half the butter in a deep frying pan over a medium–high heat until sizzling. Add the peas, spinach, mint leaves, basil and oregano and season with the nutmeg. Cook, stirring, for 3 minutes, until the spinach and mint leaves are wilted. Cool slightly.

2 Pour the spinach mixture into a food processor and process for 15 seconds. Add the mascarpone and process again for 1 minute. Transfer to a bowl and set aside.

3 Heat the oil and remaining butter in a large heavy-based saucepan over a medium heat. Add the onion, celery, garlic and thyme and cook, stirring occasionally, for 2 minutes, or until the vegetables are softened.

4 Reduce the heat, add the rice and mix to coat in oil and butter. Cook, stirring constantly, for 2–3 minutes, or until the grains are translucent. Add the vermouth and cook, stirring constantly, until it has reduced.

5 Gradually add the hot stock, a ladleful at a time. Stir constantly and add more liquid as the rice absorbs each addition. Increase the heat to medium so that the liquid bubbles. Cook for 20 minutes, or until the liquid is absorbed and the rice is creamy.

6 Stir in the spinach and mascarpone mixture and the Parmesan. Transfer to warmed plates and serve immediately.

risotto with roasted vegetables

ingredients

SERVES 4

1 tbsp olive oil

3 tbsp butter

1 small onion, finely chopped

280 g/10 oz risotto rice

1.2 litres/2 pints simmering chicken or vegetable stock

225 g/8 oz roasted vegetables, such as peppers, courgettes and aubergines, cut into chunks

salt and pepper

85 g/3 oz freshly grated Parmesan or Grana Padano cheese

2 tbsp finely chopped fresh herbs, to garnish

method

1 Heat the oil with 2 tablespoons of the butter in a deep saucepan over a medium heat until the butter has melted. Add the onion and cook, stirring occasionally, for 5 minutes, until soft and starting to turn golden. Do not brown.

2 Reduce the heat, add the rice and mix to coat in oil and butter. Cook, stirring constantly, for 2–3 minutes, or until the grains are translucent.

3 Gradually add the hot stock, a ladleful at a time. Stir constantly and add more liquid as the rice absorbs each addition. Increase the heat to medium so that the liquid bubbles. Cook for 15 minutes, then add most of the roasted vegetables, setting aside a few pieces to use as a garnish. Cook for a further 5 minutes, or until all the liquid is absorbed and the rice is creamy. Season to taste with salt and pepper.

4 Remove the risotto from the heat and add the remaining butter. Mix well, then stir in the Parmesan until it melts. Spoon the risotto onto warmed individual plates, arrange vegetables around it or on top to garnish, then sprinkle with fresh herbs and serve immediately.

risotto with artichoke hearts

ingredients

SERVES 4

225 g/8 oz canned artichoke
    hearts
1 tbsp olive oil
3 tbsp butter
1 small onion, finely chopped
10 oz/280 g risotto rice
1.2 litres/2 pints simmering
    chicken or vegetable stock
salt and pepper
85 g/3 oz freshly grated
    Parmesan or Grana
    Padano cheese
fresh flat-leaf parsley sprigs,
    to garnish

method

1 Drain the artichoke hearts, reserving the liquid, and cut them into quarters.

2 Heat the oil with 2 tablespoons of the butter in a deep saucepan over a medium heat until the butter has melted. Stir in the onion and cook gently, stirring occasionally, for 5 minutes, or until soft and starting to turn golden. Do not brown.

3 Add the rice and mix to coat in oil and butter. Cook, stirring constantly, for 2–3 minutes, or until the grains are translucent.

4 Gradually add the artichoke liquid and the hot stock, a ladleful at a time. Stir constantly and add more liquid as the rice absorbs each addition. Increase the heat to medium so that the liquid bubbles. Cook for 15 minutes, then add the artichoke hearts. Cook for a further 5 minutes, or until all the liquid is absorbed and the rice is creamy. Season to taste.

5 Remove the risotto from the heat and add the remaining butter. Mix well, then stir in the Parmesan until it melts. Season, if necessary. Spoon the risotto into warmed bowls, garnish with the parsley sprigs and serve immediately.

asparagus & sun-dried tomato risotto

ingredients

SERVES 4

1 tbsp olive oil

3 tbsp butter

1 small onion, finely chopped

6 sun-dried tomatoes, thinly
     sliced

280 g/10 oz risotto rice

1 litre/1¾ pints simmering
     vegetable stock

salt and pepper

150 ml/5 fl oz dry white wine

225 g/8 oz fresh asparagus
     spears, cooked

85 g/3 oz freshly grated
     Parmesan or Grana
     Padano cheese

thinly grated lemon rind,
     to garnish

method

1 Heat the oil with 2 tablespoons of the butter in a deep saucepan over a medium heat until the butter has melted. Stir in the onion and sun-dried tomatoes and cook, stirring occasionally, for 5 minutes until the onion is soft and starting to turn golden. Do not brown.

2 Reduce the heat, add the rice and mix to coat in oil and butter. Cook, stirring constantly, for 2–3 minutes, or until the grains are translucent. Add the wine and cook, stirring constantly, until it has reduced.

3 Gradually add the hot stock, a ladleful at a time, stirring constantly, until all the liquid is absorbed and the rice is creamy. Season to taste with salt and pepper.

4 While the risotto is cooking, cut most of the asparagus into pieces about 2.5 cm/1 inch long. Keep several spears whole for garnishing the finished dish. Carefully fold the cut pieces of asparagus into the risotto for the last 5 minutes of cooking time.

5 Remove the risotto from the heat and add the remaining butter. Mix well, then stir in the Parmesan until it melts. Spoon the risotto onto individual warmed serving dishes and garnish with the whole spears of asparagus. Sprinkle over the lemon rind and serve.

risotto primavera

ingredients

SERVES 6–8

225 g/8 oz fresh thin
    asparagus spears

4 tbsp olive oil

175 g/6 oz young green
    beans, cut into 2.5-cm/
    1-inch lengths

175 g/6 oz young courgettes,
    quartered and cut into
    2.5-cm/1-inch lengths

225 g/8 oz shelled fresh peas

1 onion, finely chopped

1–2 garlic cloves, finely
    chopped

350 g/12 oz risotto rice

1.5 litres/2³/4 pints simmering
    chicken or vegetable stock

4 spring onions, cut into
    2.5-cm/1-inch lengths

salt and pepper

55 g/2 oz butter

115 g/4 oz freshly grated
    Parmesan cheese

2 tbsp snipped fresh chives

2 tbsp shredded fresh basil

method

1 Trim the woody ends of the asparagus and cut off the tips. Cut the stems into 2.5-cm/1-inch pieces and set aside with the tips.

2 Heat 2 tablespoons of the oil in a large frying pan over a high heat until very hot. Add the asparagus, beans, courgettes and peas and stir-fry for 3–4 minutes until they are bright green and just starting to soften. Set aside.

3 Heat the remaining oil in a large heavy-based saucepan over a medium heat. Add the onion and cook, stirring occasionally, for 3 minutes, or until it starts to soften. Stir in the garlic and cook, stirring, for 30 seconds.

4 Reduce the heat, add the rice and mix to coat in oil. Cook, stirring constantly, for 2–3 minutes, or until the grains are translucent. Gradually add the hot stock, a ladleful at a time, until all but 2 tablespoons of the liquid is absorbed and the rice is creamy.

5 Stir in the stir-fried vegetables, onion mixture and spring onions with the remaining stock. Cook for 2 minutes, stirring frequently, then season to taste with salt and pepper. Stir in the butter, Parmesan, chives and basil.

6 Remove the pan from the heat. Transfer the risotto to a warmed serving dish and serve immediately.

wild mushroom risotto

ingredients

SERVES 6

55 g/2 oz dried porcini or
    morel mushrooms

about 500 g/1 lb 2 oz mixed
    fresh wild mushrooms,
    such as porcini, field
    mushrooms and
    chanterelles, halved
    if large

4 tbsp olive oil

3–4 garlic cloves, finely
    chopped

55 g/2 oz butter

1 onion, finely chopped

350 g/12 oz risotto rice

50 ml/2 fl oz dry
    white vermouth

1.2 litres/2 pints simmering
    chicken or vegetable stock

salt and pepper

115 g/4 oz freshly grated
    Parmesan cheese

4 tbsp chopped fresh
    flat-leaf parsley

method

1 Place the dried mushrooms in a heatproof bowl and add boiling water to cover. Set aside to soak for 30 minutes, then carefully lift out and pat dry. Strain the soaking liquid through a sieve lined with kitchen paper and set aside.

2 Trim the fresh mushrooms and gently brush clean. Heat 3 tablespoons of the oil in a large frying pan. Add the fresh mushrooms and stir-fry for 1–2 minutes. Add the garlic and the soaked mushrooms and cook, stirring frequently, for 2 minutes. Transfer to a plate.

3 Heat the remaining oil and half the butter in a large heavy-based saucepan. Add the onion and cook over a medium heat, stirring occasionally, for 2 minutes, until softened.

4 Reduce the heat, stir in the rice and cook, stirring constantly, for 2–3 minutes, until the grains are translucent. Add the vermouth and cook, stirring, for 1 minute until reduced.

5 Gradually add the hot stock, a ladleful at a time, until all the liquid is absorbed and the rice is creamy. Add half the reserved mushroom soaking liquid to the risotto and stir in the mushrooms. Season to taste and add more mushroom liquid, if necessary.

6 Remove the pan from the heat and stir in the remaining butter, grated Parmesan and chopped parsley. Serve immediately.

risotto with four cheeses

ingredients

SERVES 6

40 g/1½ oz unsalted butter

1 onion, finely chopped

350 g/12 oz risotto rice

200 ml/7 fl oz dry white wine

1 litre/1¾ pints simmering
vegetable stock

55 g/2 oz Gorgonzola cheese,
crumbled

55 g/2 oz freshly grated
Taleggio cheese

55 g/2 oz freshly grated
fontina cheese

55 g/2 oz freshly grated
Parmesan cheese

salt and pepper

2 tbsp chopped fresh flat-leaf
parsley, to garnish

method

1 Melt the butter in a large heavy-based
saucepan. Add the onion and cook over a low
heat, stirring occasionally, for 5 minutes, until
softened. Add the rice and cook, stirring
constantly, for 2–3 minutes, until all the grains
are thoroughly coated and glistening.

2 Add the wine and cook, stirring constantly,
until it has almost completely evaporated.
Add a ladleful of the hot stock and cook,
stirring constantly, until all the stock has
been absorbed. Continue cooking, stirring and
adding the stock, a ladleful at a time, for about
20 minutes, or until the rice is creamy and the
liquid has been absorbed.

3 Remove the pan from the heat and stir in
the Gorgonzola, Taleggio, fontina and about
one quarter of the Parmesan until melted.
Season to taste with salt and pepper. Transfer
the risotto to a warmed serving dish, sprinkle
with the remaining Parmesan, garnish with
the parsley and serve immediately.

cheese & tomato pizza

ingredients

SERVES 2

dough

225 g/8 oz plain flour, plus
extra for dusting

1 tsp salt

1 tsp easy-blend dried yeast

1 tbsp olive oil, plus extra for
brushing

6 tbsp lukewarm water

topping

6 tomatoes, thinly sliced

175 g/6 oz mozzarella
cheese, drained and
thinly sliced

salt and pepper

2 tbsp shredded fresh basil
leaves

2 tbsp olive oil

method

1 To make the pizza dough, sift the flour and salt into a bowl and stir in the yeast. Make a well in the centre and pour in the oil and water. Gradually incorporate the dry ingredients into the liquid, using a wooden spoon or floured hands.

2 Turn out the dough onto a lightly floured work surface and knead well for 5 minutes, until smooth and elastic. Return to the clean bowl, cover with lightly oiled clingfilm and set aside to rise in a warm place for about 1 hour, or until doubled in size.

3 Turn out the dough onto a lightly floured work surface and knock down. Knead briefly, then cut it in half and roll out each piece into a circle about 5 mm/1/4 inch thick. Transfer to a lightly oiled baking sheet and push up the edges with your fingers to form a small rim.

4 For the topping, arrange the tomato and mozzarella slices alternately over the pizza bases. Season to taste with salt and pepper, sprinkle with the basil and drizzle with the olive oil.

5 Bake in a preheated oven, 230°C/450°F/ Gas Mark 8, for 15–20 minutes, until the crust is crisp and the cheese has melted. Serve immediately.

desserts

Everyday Italian meals usually finish with fresh fruit, or perhaps a selection of cheeses, but when it comes to a special occasion, the Italians know how to come up with something that is as stylish as it is delicious. Usually they will head to the local *pasticceria* for an elaborate confection or, perhaps, to the *gelateria* for some of the mouthwatering ice creams for which Italy is famous.

However, there are plenty of Italian desserts that can be made at home, and this chapter has a selection of the best. Many of the most delicious desserts come from southern Italy and from the islands of Sicily and Sardinia, where fruit, nuts and honey are key ingredients. Wines, liqueurs and spirits also make a frequent appearance, especially amaretto, a distinctive almond-flavoured liqueur, and the delectably rich, sweet, Marsala wine that goes into *zabaglione*, a superb dessert that never fails to impress as it is cooked and then served immediately!

One Italian dessert that was 'invented' in the 1970s, and has since reached almost cult status, is *tiramisù*, a wonderful combination of sponge cake soaked in a mixture of rum and black coffee layered with mascarpone, the delicately flavoured cream cheese used in both sweet and savoury dishes.

chocolate & amaretto cheesecake

ingredients

SERVES 10–12

oil, for brushing
175 g/6 oz digestive biscuits
55 g/2 oz amaretti biscuits
85 g/3 oz butter

filling

225 g/8 oz plain chocolate
400 g/14 oz cream cheese
115 g/4 oz golden caster
    sugar
3 tbsp plain flour
1 tsp vanilla essence
4 eggs
300 ml/10 fl oz double cream
50 ml/2 fl oz amaretto liqueur

topping

1 tbsp amaretto liqueur
175 g/6 oz crème fraîche
crushed amaretti biscuits

method

1 Line the base of a 23-cm/9-inch springform cake tin with foil and brush the sides with oil. Place the digestive biscuits and amaretti biscuits in a plastic bag and crush with a rolling pin. Place the butter in a saucepan and heat until just melted, then stir in the crushed biscuits. Press the mixture into the bottom of the tin and chill for 1 hour.

2 To make the filling, melt the chocolate in a small heatproof bowl over a saucepan of gently simmering water, then let cool. Place the cream cheese in a bowl and beat until fluffy, then add the sugar, flour and vanilla essence and beat together until smooth. Gradually add the eggs, beating until well blended. Blend in the melted chocolate, cream and amaretto liqueur. Pour the mixture over the chilled biscuit base and bake in a preheated oven, 160°C/325°F/Gas Mark 3, for 50–60 minutes, or until set.

3 Leave the cheesecake in the oven with the door slightly ajar, until cold. Run a knife round the inside of the tin to loosen the cheesecake. Chill in the refrigerator for 2 hours, then transfer to a serving plate. To make the topping, stir the amaretto liqueur into the crème fraîche and spread over the cheesecake. Serve with a sprinkling of crushed amaretti biscuits.

ricotta cheesecake

ingredients

SERVES 6–8

pastry

175 g/6 oz plain flour, plus
extra for dusting

3 tbsp caster sugar

salt

115 g/4 oz unsalted butter,
chilled and diced

1 egg yolk

filling

450 g/1 lb ricotta cheese

125 ml/4 fl oz double cream

2 eggs, plus 1 egg yolk

85 g/3 oz caster sugar

finely grated rind of 1 lemon

finely grated rind of 1 orange

method

1 To make the pastry, sift the flour with the sugar and a pinch of salt onto a work surface and make a well in the centre. Add the diced butter and egg yolk to the well and, using your fingertips, gradually work in the flour mixture until fully incorporated. Knead very lightly.

2 Cut off about one quarter of the pastry, wrap in clingfilm and chill in the refrigerator. Press the remaining pastry into the base of a 23-cm/9-inch springform tart tin. Chill for 30 minutes.

3 To make the filling, beat the ricotta with the cream, eggs and extra egg yolk, sugar, lemon rind and orange rind. Cover with clingfilm and set aside in the refrigerator until required.

4 Prick the base of the pastry case all over with a fork. Line with foil, fill with baking beans and bake blind in a preheated oven, 190°C/375°F/Gas Mark 5, for 15 minutes. Remove from the oven and take out the foil and beans. Stand the tin on a wire rack to cool.

5 Spoon the ricotta mixture into the pastry case and level the surface. Roll out the reserved pastry on a lightly floured work surface, cut it into strips and arrange over the filling in a lattice pattern. Brush the ends with water so they stick.

6 Bake in the oven for 30–35 minutes, until the top of the cheesecake is golden and the filling has set. Cool on a wire rack before lifting off the side of the tin. Serve cut into wedges.

almond cake

ingredients

SERVES 12–14

butter, for greasing

3 eggs, separated

140 g/5 oz caster sugar

55 g/2 oz potato flour

140 g/5 oz almonds,
    blanched, peeled and
    finely chopped

finely grated rind of 1 orange

125 ml/4 fl oz orange juice

salt

icing sugar, for dusting

method

1 Generously grease a round 20-cm/8-inch springform cake tin. Beat the egg yolks with the sugar in a medium bowl until pale and thick and the mixture leaves a ribbon trail when the whisk is lifted. Stir in the potato flour, almonds, orange rind and orange juice.

2 Whisk the egg whites with a pinch of salt in another bowl until stiff. Gently fold the whites into the egg yolk mixture.

3 Pour the mixture into the pan and bake in a preheated oven, 170°C/325°F/Gas Mark 3$^{1/2}$, for 50–60 minutes, until golden and just firm to the touch. Turn out onto a wire rack to cool. Sift over a little icing sugar to decorate before serving.

tuscan christmas cake

ingredients

SERVES 12–14

115 g/4 oz hazelnuts
115 g/4 oz almonds
85 g/3 oz candied peel
55 g/2 oz dried apricots,
    finely chopped
55 g/2 oz candied pineapple,
    finely chopped
grated rind of 1 orange
55 g/2 oz plain flour
2 tbsp cocoa powder
1 tsp ground cinnamon
¼ tsp ground coriander
¼ tsp freshly grated nutmeg
¼ tsp ground cloves
115 g/4 oz caster sugar
175 g/6 oz honey
icing sugar, to decorate

method

1 Line a 20-cm/8-inch springform cake tin with baking paper. Spread out the hazelnuts on a baking sheet and toast in a preheated oven, 180°C/350°F/Gas Mark 4, for 10 minutes, until golden brown. Pour them onto a tea towel and rub off the skins.

2 Spread out the almonds on a baking sheet and toast in the oven for 7–10 minutes, until golden. Reduce the oven temperature to 150°C/300°F/Gas Mark 2. Chop all the nuts and place in a large bowl.

3 Add the candied peel, apricots, pineapple and orange rind to the nuts and mix well. Sift together the flour, cocoa powder, cinnamon, coriander, nutmeg and cloves into the bowl and mix well.

4 Put the sugar and honey in a saucepan and stir over a low heat until the sugar has dissolved. Bring to the boil and cook for 5 minutes, until thickened and starting to darken. Stir in the nut mixture and remove from the heat.

5 Spoon the mixture into the prepared cake tin and level the surface with the back of a damp spoon. Bake in the oven for 1 hour, then transfer to a wire rack to cool in the tin.

6 Carefully remove the cake from the tin and peel off the baking paper. Just before serving, dredge the top with icing sugar. Cut into thin wedges to serve.

chestnut & chocolate terrine

ingredients

SERVES 6

200 ml/7 fl oz double cream

115 g/4 oz plain chocolate, melted and cooled

100 ml/3^{1}/$_{2}$ fl oz rum

1 packet rectangular, plain, sweet biscuits

225 g/8 oz canned sweetened chestnut purée

cocoa powder, for dusting

icing sugar, to decorate

method

1 Line a 450-g/1-lb loaf tin with clingfilm. Place the cream in a bowl and whip lightly until soft peaks form. Using a spatula, fold in the cooled chocolate.

2 Place the rum in a shallow dish. Lightly dip 4 biscuits into the rum and arrange on the bottom of the tin. Repeat with 4 more biscuits. Spread half the chocolate cream over the biscuits. Make another layer of 8 biscuits dipped in rum and spread the chestnut purée over them, followed by another layer of biscuits. Spread over the remaining chocolate cream and top with a final layer of 8 biscuits. Cover with clingfilm and chill for 8 hours, or preferably overnight.

3 Turn the terrine out onto a large serving dish. Dust with cocoa powder. Cut strips of paper and place these randomly on top of the terrine. Sift over icing sugar, then carefully remove the paper. To serve, dip a sharp knife in hot water, dry it and use it to cut the terrine into slices.

tiramisù

ingredients

SERVES 8

butter, for greasing

3 eggs

140 g/5 oz golden caster
    sugar

90 g/3¼ oz self-raising flour

1 tbsp cocoa powder

150 ml/5 fl oz cold black
    coffee

2 tbsp rum

2 tsp cocoa powder,
    to decorate

filling

375 g/13 oz mascarpone
    cheese

225 ml/8 fl oz fresh custard

55 g/2 oz golden caster sugar

100 g/3½ oz plain chocolate,
    grated

method

1 To make the cake, grease a 20-cm/8-inch round cake tin with butter and line with baking paper. Place the eggs and sugar in a large bowl and beat together until thick and light. Sift the flour and cocoa powder over the batter and fold in gently. Spoon the batter into the tin and bake in a preheated oven, 180°C/350°F/ Gas Mark 4, for 30 minutes, or until the cake springs back when pressed gently in the centre. Let stand in the tin for 5 minutes, then turn out onto a wire rack to cool.

2 Place the black coffee and rum in a bowl or cup, mix together and set aside. To make the filling, place the mascarpone cheese in a large bowl and beat until soft. Stir in the custard, then gradually add the sugar, beating constantly. Stir in the grated chocolate.

3 Cut the cake horizontally into 3 layers and place 1 layer on a serving plate. Sprinkle with one third of the coffee mixture, then cover with one third of the mascarpone mixture. Repeat the layers, finishing with a topping of the mascarpone mixture. Chill in the refrigerator for 3 hours. Sift over the cocoa powder before serving.

italian chocolate christmas pudding

ingredients

SERVES 10

115 g/4 oz mixed candied
    fruit, chopped
55 g/2 oz raisins
grated rind of $\frac{1}{2}$ orange
3 tbsp orange juice
3 tbsp single cream
350 g/12 oz plain
    chocolate, chopped
115 g/4 oz cream cheese
115 g/4 oz amaretti biscuits,
    roughly broken into pieces
butter, for greasing

to serve

125 ml/4 fl oz whipping
    cream
2 tbsp amaretto liqueur
25 g/1 oz plain chocolate,
    grated

method

1 Place the candied fruit, raisins, orange rind and juice in a bowl and mix together. Put the single cream and chocolate in a saucepan and heat gently until the chocolate has melted. Stir until smooth, then stir in the fruit mixture. Remove the pan from the heat and set aside to cool.

2 Place the cream cheese and a little of the chocolate mixture in a large bowl and beat together until smooth, then stir in the remaining chocolate mixture. Stir in the broken amaretti biscuits. Pour into an 850-ml/1½-pint ovenproof bowl greased with butter, cover with clingfilm and chill in the refrigerator overnight.

3 To serve, turn the pudding out onto a chilled serving plate. Pour the whipping cream into a bowl and add the amaretto liqueur. Whip lightly until slightly thickened. Pour some of the cream over the pudding and sprinkle grated chocolate over the top. Serve with the remaining cream.

sicilian ricotta cake

ingredients

SERVES 4

Genoa sponge cake

6 eggs, separated

200 g/7 oz caster sugar

85 g/3 oz self-raising flour

85 g/3 oz cornflour

filling

500 g/1 lb 2 oz ricotta cheese

200 g/7 oz caster sugar

600 ml/1 pint Maraschino
    liqueur

85 g/3 oz plain chocolate

200 g/7 oz mixed candied
    peel, diced

to decorate

300 ml/10 fl oz double cream

glacé cherries

angelica

candied fruit

flaked almonds

method

1 Line a 25-cm/10-inch springform cake tin with baking paper. Beat the egg yolks with the sugar until pale and frothy. In a separate, spotlessly clean bowl, whisk the whites until stiff peaks form. Gently fold the whites into the egg yolk mixture with a figure-of-eight action.

2 Sift together the flour and cornflour into a bowl, then sift into the egg mixture and gently fold in. Pour the mixture into the cake tin and level the surface. Bake in a preheated oven, 180°C/350°F/Gas Mark 4, for 30 minutes, until springy to the touch. Turn out onto a wire rack, remove the lining paper and cool completely.

3 For the filling, combine the ricotta, sugar and 400 ml/14 fl oz of the Maraschino in a bowl, beating well. Chop the chocolate with a knife and stir it into the mixture with the candied fruit.

4 Cut the sponge cake into 1 cm/1/2 inch wide strips and use some of it to line the base and sides of a 900-g/2-lb loaf tin. Set aside the remaining slices. Spoon the ricotta mixture into the tin and level the surface. Cover with the reserved sponge cake. Drizzle the remaining Maraschino over the top, then chill overnight.

5 Turn the cake out onto a serving plate. Whisk the cream until stiff and coat the top and sides of the cake. Decorate with the cherries, angelica, candied fruit and almonds.

lemon granita

ingredients

SERVES 4

450 ml/15 fl oz water
115 g/4 oz sugar
225 ml/8 fl oz lemon juice
grated rind of 1 lemon

method

1 Heat the water in a heavy-based saucepan over a low heat. Add the sugar and stir until it has completely dissolved. Bring to the boil, remove the pan from the heat and set aside to cool.

2 Stir the lemon juice and rind into the syrup. Pour the mixture into a freezerproof container and place in the freezer for 3–4 hours.

3 To serve, remove the container from the freezer and dip the base into hot water. Turn out the ice block and chop roughly, then place in a food processor and process until it forms small crystals (granita means 'granular'). Spoon into sundae glasses and serve immediately.

zucotto

ingredients

SERVES 6

115 g/4 oz soft margarine,
plus extra for greasing
100 g/3^{1}/$_{2}$ oz self-raising flour
2 tbsp cocoa powder
^{1}/$_{2}$ tsp baking powder
115 g/4 oz golden caster
sugar
2 eggs, beaten
3 tbsp brandy
2 tbsp Kirsch

filling

300 ml/10 fl oz double cream
25 g/1 oz icing sugar, sifted
55 g/2 oz toasted almonds,
chopped
225 g/8 oz black cherries,
stoned
55 g/2 oz plain chocolate,
finely chopped

to decorate

1 tbsp cocoa powder
1 tbsp icing sugar
fresh cherries

method

1 Grease a 30 x 23-cm/12 x 9-inch Swiss roll tin with margarine and line with baking paper. Sift the flour, cocoa and baking powder into a bowl. Add the sugar, margarine and eggs. Beat together until well mixed, then spoon into the prepared tin. Bake in a preheated oven, 190°C/375°F/Gas Mark 5, for 15–20 minutes, or until well risen and firm to the touch. Let stand in the tin for 5 minutes, then turn out onto a wire rack to cool.

2 Using the rim of a 1.2-litre/2-pint ovenproof bowl as a guide, cut a circle from the cake and set aside. Line the bowl with clingfilm, then with the remaining cake, cutting it as necessary. Place the brandy and Kirsch in a small bowl and mix together. Sprinkle over the cake, including the reserved circle.

3 To make the filling, pour the cream into a separate bowl and add the icing sugar. Whip until thick, then fold in the almonds, cherries and chocolate. Fill the sponge mould with the cream mixture and press the cake circle on top. Cover with a plate and a weight and chill in the refrigerator for 6–8 hours or overnight. When ready to serve, turn the zucotto out onto a serving plate. Decorate with cocoa and icing sugar, sifted over in alternating segments, and a few cherries.

chestnut mousse

ingredients

SERVES 6

450 g/1 lb sweet chestnuts
300 ml/10 fl oz milk
1 bay leaf
2.5-cm/2-inch cinnamon
    stick
175 g/6 oz caster sugar
2 large eggs yolks
1/2 tsp vanilla essence
4 tbsp dark rum
150 ml/5 fl oz double cream,
    plus extra to decorate
butter, for greasing

method

1 Cut a slit in the rounded side of the shell of each chestnut. Place them in a large saucepan, add cold water to cover, bring to the boil and boil for 5 minutes. Remove with a slotted spoon. When cool enough to handle, but still warm, remove the shells and the inner skins.

2 Place the chestnuts in a clean saucepan. Add the milk, bay leaf, cinnamon and half the sugar. Bring to the boil, stirring, then reduce the heat, cover and simmer gently, stirring occasionally, for 40 minutes, or until the chestnuts are very tender. Set aside to cool.

3 Remove and discard the bay leaf and cinnamon stick from the pan then transfer the contents to a food processor or blender. Process to a smooth purée.

4 Beat the egg yolks and remaining sugar until pale and fluffy and the whisk leaves a trail when lifted. Stir in the vanilla essence and rum, then gently fold in the chestnut purée. Whip the cream in a separate bowl until it forms stiff peaks. Gently fold it into the chestnut mixture.

5 Spoon the mixture into 6 individual ovenproof moulds lightly greased with butter. Stand the moulds on a baking sheet and bake in a preheated oven, 180°C/350°F/Gas Mark 4, for 10–15 minutes, until just set. Cool to room temperature. To serve, turn out the moulds onto individual plates and pipe a border of whipped cream around the base of each one.

zabaglione

ingredients

SERVES 4

4 egg yolks

60 g/2¹/₄ oz caster sugar

5 tbsp Marsala

amaretti biscuits, to serve

method

1 Whisk the egg yolks with the sugar in a heatproof bowl for about 1 minute.

2 Gently whisk in the Marsala. Set the bowl over a pan of barely simmering water and whisk vigorously for 10–15 minutes, until thick, creamy and foamy.

3 Immediately pour into serving glasses and serve with amaretti biscuits.

chocolate zabaglione

ingredients

SERVES 4

4 egg yolks

4 tbsp caster sugar

50 g/1¾ oz plain chocolate

125 ml/4 fl oz Marsala wine

cocoa powder, for dusting

amaretti biscuits, to serve

method

1 Place the egg yolks and caster sugar in a large glass bowl and, using an electric whisk, whisk together until the mixture is very pale.

2 Grate the chocolate finely and, using a spatula, fold into the egg mixture. Fold the Marsala wine into the chocolate mixture.

3 Place the bowl over a pan of gently simmering water and set the electric whisk on the lowest speed or use a balloon whisk. Cook gently, whisking constantly, until the mixture thickens. Do not overcook or the mixture will curdle.

4 Spoon the hot mixture into 4 warmed glass dishes or coffee cups and dust with cocoa. Serve as soon as possible, while it is warm, light and fluffy, with amaretti biscuits.

mascarpone creams

ingredients

SERVES 4

115 g/4 oz amaretti biscuits,
    crushed

4 tbsp amaretto or
    Maraschino

4 eggs, separated

55 g/2 oz caster sugar

225 g/8 oz mascarpone
    cheese

toasted flaked almonds,
    to decorate

method

1 Place the amaretti crumbs in a bowl, add the amaretto or Maraschino and set aside to soak.

2 Meanwhile, beat the egg yolks with the caster sugar until pale and thick. Fold in the mascarpone and soaked biscuit crumbs.

3 Whisk the egg whites in a separate, spotlessly clean bowl until stiff, then gently fold into the cheese mixture. Divide the mascarpone cream between 4 serving dishes and chill for 1–2 hours. Sprinkle with the flaked almonds just before serving.

chilled chocolate dessert

ingredients

SERVES 4–6

225 g/8 oz mascarpone
cheese

2 tbsp finely ground coffee
beans

25 g/1 oz icing sugar

85 g/3 oz unsweetened
chocolate, finely grated

350 ml/12 fl oz double
cream, plus extra
to decorate

Marsala, to serve

method

1 Beat the mascarpone cheese with the coffee and icing sugar until thoroughly combined.

2 Set aside 4 teaspoons of the grated chocolate and stir the remainder into the cheese mixture with 5 tablespoons of the unwhipped cream.

3 Whisk the remaining cream until it forms soft peaks. Stir 1 tablespoon of the mascarpone mixture into the cream to slacken it, then fold the cream into the remaining mascarpone mixture with a figure-of-eight action.

4 Spoon the mixture into a freezerproof container and place in the freezer for about 3 hours.

5 To serve, scoop the chocolate dessert into sundae glasses and drizzle with a little Marsala. Top with the extra cream, whipped, and decorate with the reserved grated chocolate. Serve immediately.

cappuccino soufflé puddings

ingredients

SERVES 4

butter, for greasing

2 tbsp golden caster sugar,
    plus extra for coating

6 tbsp whipping cream

2 tsp instant espresso coffee
    granules

2 tbsp Kahlua

3 large eggs, separated,
    plus 1 extra egg white

150 g/5^1/2 oz plain chocolate,
    melted and cooled

cocoa powder, for dusting

vanilla ice cream, to serve

method

1 Lightly grease the sides of 6 x 175-ml/6-fl oz ramekins with butter and coat with caster sugar. Place the ramekins on a baking sheet.

2 Place the cream in a small, heavy-based saucepan and heat gently. Stir in the coffee until it has dissolved, then stir in the Kahlua. Divide the coffee mixture between the prepared ramekins.

3 Place the egg whites in a clean, greasefree bowl and whisk until soft peaks form, then gradually whisk in the sugar until stiff but not dry. Stir the egg yolks and melted chocolate together in a separate bowl, then stir in a little of the whisked egg whites. Gradually fold in the remaining egg whites.

4 Divide the mixture between the dishes. Bake in a preheated oven, 190°C/375°F/Gas Mark 5 for 15 minutes or until just set. Dust with cocoa powder and serve immediately with vanilla ice cream.

coffee panna cotta with chocolate sauce

ingredients

SERVES 6

oil, for brushing

600 ml/1 pint double cream

1 vanilla pod

55 g/2 oz golden caster sugar

2 tsp instant espresso coffee
    granules, dissolved in
    4 tbsp water

2 tsp powdered gelatine

chocolate-covered coffee
    beans, to serve

sauce

150 ml/5 fl oz single cream

55 g/2 oz plain chocolate,
    melted

method

1 Lightly brush 6 x 150-ml/5-fl oz moulds with oil. Place the cream in a pan. Split the vanilla pod and scrape the black seeds into the cream. Add the vanilla pod and the sugar, then heat gently until almost boiling. Strain the cream into a heatproof bowl and set aside. Place the coffee in a small heatproof bowl, sprinkle on the gelatine and let stand for 5 minutes, or until spongy. Set the bowl over a saucepan of gently simmering water until the gelatine has dissolved.

2 Stir a little of the vanilla cream into the gelatine mixture, then stir the gelatine mixture into the remainder of the cream. Divide the mixture between the prepared moulds and cool, then chill in the refrigerator for 8 hours, or overnight.

3 To make the sauce, place one quarter of the cream in a bowl and stir in the melted chocolate. Gradually stir in the remaining cream, reserving 1 tablespoon. To serve the panna cotta, dip the base of the moulds briefly into hot water and turn out onto 6 dessert plates. Pour the chocolate cream round the edge. Dot drops of the reserved cream onto the sauce and feather it with a cocktail stick. Decorate with chocolate-covered coffee beans to serve.

marsala cherries

ingredients

SERVES 4

140 g/5 oz caster sugar

thinly pared rind of 1 lemon

5-cm/2-inch piece of
   cinnamon stick

225 ml/8 fl oz water

225 ml/8 fl oz Marsala

900 g/2 lb Morello cherries,
   stoned

150 ml/5 fl oz double cream

method

1 Put the sugar, lemon rind, cinnamon stick, water and Marsala in a heavy-based saucepan and bring to the boil, stirring constantly. Reduce the heat and simmer for 5 minutes. Remove the cinnamon stick.

2 Add the Morello cherries, cover and simmer gently for 10 minutes. Using a slotted spoon, transfer the cherries to a bowl.

3 Return the pan to the heat and bring to the boil over a high heat. Boil for 3–4 minutes, until thick and syrupy. Pour the syrup over the cherries and set aside to cool, then chill for at least 1 hour.

4 Whisk the cream until stiff peaks form. Divide the cherries and syrup between 4 individual dishes or glasses, top with the cream and serve.